The Worlds of Ernest Thompson Seton

ADVENTURES IN THE WILD

The Worlds of Ernest Thompson Seton

ADVENTURES IN THE WILD

Edited by John G. Samson

ARROWOOD PRESS

New York

The editor is grateful to the following for supplying photographs, art, published and unpublished writings of Ernest Thompson Seton appearing in this volume: Mrs. R. Dee Barber, Santa Fe, New Mexico; the Seton Museum, Cimarron, New Mexico; the Boy Scouts of America; Field & Stream magazine; The American Museum of Natural History; and the New York Zoological Society. The editor also wishes to thank Dick Kent, who photographed the Seton collection in New Mexico.

First published by Arrowood Press in 1990.

Arrowood Press
A division of Budget Book Service, Inc.
386 Park Avenue South
New York, NY 10016

Published by arrangement with Alfred A. Knopf, Inc.

Library of Congress Catalog Card Number: 76-13711
ISBN: 0-88486-034-5

Printed in China.

TO VICTORIA
Without Whose Constant Assistance
This Book Would Never Have Seen
the
Light of Day

CONTENTS

ILLUSTRATIONS

More years ago than I care to specify, my older brother, Ed, received a set of books dealing with animals, woodcraft, and outdoor adventure. The gift probably marked his entry into the Boy Scouts. Word about the fascinating treasures within the volumes, each with its simulated birchbark cover, began to filter down to number-two boy, and I was soon off on vicarious adventures with Coaly-Bay, Foam, and Rolf, among many other furred, feathered, and human heroes. Of course, the spirited drawings, diagrams, and cartoons surrounding the text area caught my eye, for I was already infected with my lifelong infatuation with animal representation in any form.

My response to Seton at that time of first exposure was, to my best recollection, one of fascination with the animal characters he created and portrayed. I don't think I was wise enough then to understand the sophisticated simplicity of his art. I only knew that his wild heroes were real and alive, and that, whatever dilemma they found themselves in, I was keenly interested in their survival. That the drawings and paintings contributed to my involvement in the stories (along with many thousands of other youngsters) was a factor I accepted without much thought. My own animal doodling was instinctive, and Seton's body of graphics, done in an entirely different way than anything I'd seen, added new fuel to the fire of my ambition to be a wildlife illustrator.

How does one evaluate Seton as an artist? If ever there was a versatile man, he was it. One can no more separate the drawing and painting from the writing, lecturing, or research into ancient woodcraft skills than one can examine the off hind leg of a stag and properly assess the appearance and nature of the whole animal. But since my competence, such as it is, lies in the area of animal art, it is from that vantage point that I will attempt an appraisal.

It is an exercise in foolishness, I think, to compare Seton with Audubon, Louis Agassiz Fuertes, Carl Rungius—or Paul Bransom and Livingston Bull, for that matter. These were full-time practitioners, and all portrayed wildlife with great skill. Seton's effort—with the exception of some finished studies, many of which appear in this volume—was to capture an essence. His drawings, so apparently simple, are full of the character of the object depicted. Anyone in possession of his *Studies in the Art Anatomy of Animals* can see the serious attention Seton paid to the underlying structure of the creatures he so blithely and "effortlessly" translated into brush-and-ink.

Someone once asked a knowledgeable baseball man what was so special about Joe DiMaggio. Couldn't Charlie Keller do everything that Joe did? Possibly, was the answer, but Joe made it all look easy. So too with Seton. His drawings, guileless and devoid of fuss, truly illuminate the yarns they are designed to augment. The halftones, too, though less vivid bear, I think, Seton's stamp of authority and help us to visualize clearly his protagonists as he saw them.

Perhaps Jack Samson's book, with its comprehensive approach to his subject, Ernest Thompson Seton, will reawaken a curiosity among young readers in this versatile man's exciting and informative view of an earlier America, one not blighted by smog and urban sprawl, one we shared more equitably with our wild neighbors, one in which the lore of the Indian was still of practical use. If this is so, if *The Worlds of Ernest Thompson Seton* does rekindle interest in this creative man, then I for one will be very pleased. And the magic of those stories and the drawings that danced around the margins of the pages of the Birchbark series will continue to excite the heart and the imagination.

BOB KUHN

The Worlds of Ernest Thompson Seton

ADVENTURES IN THE WILD

Ernest Thompson Seton was no mere naturalist. He was a gifted painter and a sketch artist far ahead of his time—highly creative in Canada, Europe, and the United States from the 1880's until shortly before his death in 1946.

A driven man, Seton turned out an incredible amount of work for one lifetime. His forty-odd books alone would have been more than enough for almost any writer, but in addition he was a ceaseless researcher, scientist, lecturer, traveler, and artist. His four-volume *Lives of Game Animals* would have been a massive work for the average writer. At the peak of his career he was considered by such notables as William Hornaday, Theodore Roosevelt, and Frank Chapman, and by the American Museum of Natural History, to be the best all-round animal and bird artist in America. By the early 1900's Seton had received almost every honor that could be bestowed upon a naturalist.

As if that were not enough, his writing was narrative, and he hit upon a knack of telling a story that appealed not only to children but to people of all ages who love the outdoors and wild creatures. More than half a century before Walt Disney and the invention of the animated movie cartoon, Seton brought animal characters to life through his writing and sketching. Silverspot the crow, Lobo the wolf, Ragglylug the cottontail rabbit, and Wahb the huge grizzly bear are as alive today in the pages of his books and on his sketch pads as when they were household names in America, Canada, and Europe before the turn of the century.

Like Disney, he often attributed far too many human traits to wild creatures, but that is forgivable in a man who was writing books to sell. The demand of the children's-book market was there. Seton simply saw it and filled the need. And in a strange way I believe Seton really wished wild animals were like that—tender, courageous, loving, and loyal—much as he knew domesticated animals could be.

But, on the other side of the coin, he was a practical naturalist who knew that nature is real and that nature is cruel. He knew only too well that in the real world of nature the predator kills and the weak die. He knew, too, that the doe would push her spring fawn away from the last remaining food as deer yarded up in the deep winter snow—because that is the way nature is. The strong survive to breed—keeping the species strong. He was a hunter himself, although in his books he professed to detest sport hunting because he knew that attitude sold books, particularly children's books. Seton was an excellent shot with a shotgun; he killed and collected birds all his life both for scientific study of skins and to sketch and paint. In the old files of his beloved Camp Fire Club of America at Chappaqua, New York, which he helped to found, are records of awards he won for successfully stalking and killing such big-game animals as bull elk and buck antelope.

And yet Seton saw the end of the "endless" buffalo herds and decried the needless slaughter of wildlife. He saw the danger in commercial hunting and argued for federal and international laws setting legal bag limits and restricted hunting seasons to prevent market hunting. He was deeply annoyed at the polluters and despoilers of his day and cautioned that care was needed to preserve wildlife in America and Canada.

Conservationist, ecologist, environmentalist, preservationist—all these terms are flung about today at random by those attempting to categorize someone concerned about nature and wildlife. Seton was a conservationist and a realist in the days when there were no catch-all phrases for those who worried about America's dwindling wildlife resources. He was intimately concerned with wild things because he grew up inside nature. From the time he was a small boy in Manitoba he had immersed himself in wild living things. Burning with desire to know everything about all wild creatures, he drove himself to learn all there was to learn.

Today we have libraries filled with information about our wild creatures, but there were few books available for him to read, fewer paintings for him to study, and almost no teachers for him to seek out. The few naturalists about—Burroughs, Agassiz, and Audubon—were either too far distant from him or too busy to be concerned with a boy from the Canadian provinces.

Fortunately for the world—although Seton would not have agreed at the time—his father grew tired of seeing his son following what seemed an impractical dream. He took him from his boyhood woods and wildlife and sent him to London's Royal Academy of Art to become an artist. Seton had a natural talent for sketching and did well at his studies. Some of his sketches done at art school are shown in this book and point to a talent already flowering. Some of his best oil paintings were done during his art-school days and shortly afterward—such as his famous sleeping wolf, which hung on gallery walls for years and was done from a captive wolf in the Paris zoo.

Strangely enough, Seton did not really like to paint. He considered it a chore, and although he was very good at it, he would far rather sketch. He was a tireless sketch artist and a ceaseless chronicler of what he saw in nature. It was this combination—faithfully put down in thirty-odd diaries— that allowed him to write his books. Early in his career he was told to keep a daily diary of events, and he did so until his death. These diaries are today the property of the American Museum of Natural History and may be viewed there.

The days and nights on the teeming plains of Manitoba in the 1880's filled him with an anguish of frustration. There were scores of birds for which he had no names. There were flowering plants with only local names which he could not classify. Small game animals and rodents were everywhere— as were insects, reptiles, and amphibians which he could collect and sketch, but which—for him—had no names. Each day became a full, bursting thing for him, and the seasons melted into one another only too quickly as he tried to absorb it all. He was not healthy as a school-boy and his eyesight was poor from poring over notes and books and sketching constantly. He grew more healthy as he reached his twenties, however, and after undergoing a hernia operation he became a sturdy young man with boundless energy.

His was a fascination with everything in nature, from the blizzards that buried the Canadian provinces in the winter to the long simmering days of summer, when the world was alive with a thousand sights and voices of the wild. Seton's sketches are authentic because not only was he a natural sketch artist, but he had taken the time to learn anatomy—as far too few art students do today. A glance at some of the "art anatomy of animals" plates he did in 1896 will show one why even his preliminary sketches were accurate. He knew where each muscle, bone, and tendon belonged—not only in domesticated animals and birds but in wild creatures. He was *concerned* with the proper scientific name for everything, from plants to rocks, and this concern accounts for his exacting backgrounds and landscapes.

The identification drawings of waterfowl on the water, done in 1882, and the in-flight color charts for identification of birds of prey are still in use. They were utilized in the 1930's by ornithologist Roger Tory Peterson in his fine field guides to birds and in other books by later naturalists.

One wonders whether, if Seton had known the extent of his undertaking, he would have been as anxious to tackle the task. His *Life Histories of Northern Animals,* published in 1909, was a good but incomplete job of covering what he chose to call "game animals." Much of this book was incorporated into his later *Lives of Game Animals,* for which he gained so much recognition. "Game animals" is a loose term and somewhat unscientific. By today's definition the term means animals which are hunted legally for food or sport. They are covered by specific state and federal hunting regulations. Many of the "game" species Seton concerned himself about have never been hunted much for either purpose. It is difficult to imagine anyone hunting a shrew or a mole for food or sport, but Seton devoted writing and art to such wild creatures.

Certain animals had a special fascination for Seton. Wolves, coyotes, and the big bears particularly interested him. He was to spend his life writing about and sketching wolves—indeed, even incorporating a wolf footprint into his signature. All this stemmed from his conviction that he was related to an ancient Scottish hunter who reputedly killed the last wolf in the British Isles. However, it was not this alone which caused him to spend much of his life studying wolves. He really felt a brother to wild wolves—in a metaphysical way. He could spend hours or days studying and sketching a beaver or a caribou, but it was wolves that captured his imagination most. His experiences on a cattle ranch in northeastern New Mexico in 1893 cast the die for his lifelong interest in them. He was caught up in trying to trap some huge, wise, and immensely strong timber wolves that were killing an enormous number of cattle in the area. It was probably his insight into the intelligence and fearlessness of these animals that made him a wolf-lover all the rest of his life. It is certainly where his book *Lobo, King of the Currumpaw* came from—a recounting of the chase and capture of both a giant killer wolf and its white mate, Blanca. The white mate was used to decoy Lobo to capture after all other means had failed. Seton never forgot the way the giant

wolf refused to eat after capture and simply stared into space until it died. The skin of the giant wolf hangs today on a wall of the Seton Museum in Cimarron, New Mexico, where thousands of persons go each year to view Seton's paintings and sketches. The museum was built by the Boy Scouts of America, an organization of which Seton was co-founder.

Seton was a tireless romantic all his life, and much of his writing is centered around the age-old conflict between good and evil, the strong and the weak, the cowardly and the brave. His damsels were always fair and desperately in need of defending, and his knights were invariably in shining armor—regardless of how bloody. His bears chose to die a noble death in a gas-filled valley rather than live to an old age that made them susceptible to defeat in battle. His heroic mountain rams hurled themselves over cliffs before letting the red-eyed hunter cut them down in ignominy. His mother grouse and mother rabbits threw themselves into frozen streams and before slavering hounds to save their trembling young. That's the way his young readers wanted it, true, but it is entirely possible that Seton really believed in such a life style. All his writings to the young in his scouting handbooks, his books on woodcraft, and his rules for games read like a bit of the playing fields of Eton. There was never any compromise, and one simply did the right thing. One can see his fine hand

Portrait of Seton at the peak of his career, taken in New York in 1906. Here the romantic aspect of Seton's passion for the outdoors emerges from both pose and garb.

in many of the rules which to this day govern conduct at the Camp Fire Club of America—still active in Chappaqua, New York. Members join for good fellowship, yes, but they must meet certain rigid requirements and they are expected to behave like gentlemen at all times—à la Seton.

As Seton's romanticism sometimes colored what he saw in nature, he was often guilty of anthropomorphism. Because he talked animals and birds to everyone he met, he often collected yarns—old woodsmen's tales, sometimes—that have caused many general readers, to say nothing of mammalogists and ornithologists, to raise dubious eyebrows now and then and to think of Ernest Thompson Seton as a "naturalist" of the old school. And, of course, modern scientists in the biological disciplines give naturalists short shrift. On the other hand, it should be remembered that many of those same men and women who study animals and birds under the rigors of scientific controls were first attracted to nature by the charm, enthusiasm, and devotion of Seton's writings, drawings, and paintings.

Seton's other obsession was the Indian. From boyhood he admired the Canadian Indians greatly and emulated their way of life in the wild. His books *Two Little Savages* and *Rolf in the Woods* were patterned after Indian woodcraft and woods lore. When he began his travels to the West in the 1920's and 1930's, he spent a great deal of time with the Plains Indians and finally the Pueblo tribes of New Mexico, where he moved in 1930. Seton had two great hates in life: Saint Paul and General George Armstrong Custer. He disliked Saint Paul because he considered him anti-female and Seton was, above all else, a champion of womanhood. Custer was an Indian-hater in Seton's eyes and that alone made him a target of wrath. Seton never forgave Custer for the battle of the Little Big Horn (though Custer hardly needed forgiveness after *that* encounter) and he made it a point to travel to the burial place of Chief Sitting Bull in 1937 and have his picture taken standing beside the grave, hat in hand and face averted.

Much of Seton's art is lost to the general public. Some of it undoubtedly hangs in private collections, and a considerable amount has been misplaced or discarded in the last hundred years by publishing companies. Seton illustrated a number of bird and animal books, plus hundreds of magazine stories, and the periodicals and publishing houses of those days bought all rights to art as well as manuscript. Seton's sketches do turn up periodically in print shops and at auctions, and there is a good chance of picking one up if a collector continues searching. His early sketches and paintings were signed just with his initials—"ETS" for Ernest Thompson Seton. He also signed many as "Ernest S. Thompson"—his family name until he changed it officially to Seton in 1901. The reason for the name change is that Seton was never particularly fond of his father, a stern man, the father of ten sons and one adopted daughter— and one who, Seton thought, was at times brusque and unkind to his wife. Seton worshiped his mother, and a host of amateur psychiatrists could probably make much of this and the fact that he tended to put women on a pedestal all his life. However, the family name was Seton in the years when Scottish clans battled constantly and took sides in various English wars. Apparently, the Seton clan was on the losing side in the Stuart rebellion of 1745 and the family, in order to avoid retribution, had to flee south to England, where Seton's grandfather hastily changed his name to Thompson.

Seton was born in 1860 in South Shields, England, where his father was a prosperous shipbuilder. However, the family fortunes changed some years later and the Thompsons moved to Canada to begin a new life. When Seton was finally on his own and began to enjoy some success as an artist, he changed his name back to Seton. During the rest of his life he frequently alluded to his origin as a member of the Seton clan. He was a Canadian by nationality until becoming an American citizen in 1930.

Seton was married in 1896 to a socialite, Grace Gallatin. Their daughter, Ann, was born in 1904 and became, as Anya Seton, the author of such fine novels as *The Turquoise, Katherine, Avalon,* and *Green Darkness.*

Grace herself was something of a book designer and quite a good writer—helping to design some of Seton's early books and writing several of her own. Much of Seton's social life of those days was spent in and around New York; he and Grace maintained a town house in Manhattan and homes in New Jersey and Cos Cob, Connecticut. Seton was friend and confidant of other well-known naturalists and scientists of his day: William Hornaday, director of the New York Zoological Society; Frank Chapman, of the American Museum of Natural History; Daniel Carter Beard, another fine illustrator and outdoor enthusiast, who, with Seton, was a co-founder of the Boy Scouts of America; and such other notables of the times as Theodore Roosevelt and Buffalo Bill Cody. He was much sought after as an illustrator of outdoor books and as a lecturer.

His marriage to Grace Gallatin Seton ended in divorce, and Seton was to marry his longtime secretary, Julia Buttree, in 1935, after leaving the East and moving to Santa Fe. They later adopted a daughter, Beulah, who still lives in his huge "castle" of a home in Santa Fe, where much of his art hangs today. The bulk of his remaining paintings and sketches is on display at the Seton Museum in Cimarron.

It was the Manitoba prairie years that shaped Seton's life as a naturalist. There he first became aware of his abilities as a sketch artist and, also for the first time, knew the joy of strength and health. He became a tireless note taker and an incessant seeker of more of nature's wonders to sketch on the pages of his diaries.

No songbird was shy enough to escape his scrutiny nor any gopher quick enough to avoid his sharp eye and pencil. It was a time of recording bird songs and sprouting wildflowers, flight patterns of waterfowl and the tracks of the lynx and snowshoe rabbit.

From the volumes of notes came his first books and pamphlets: *Life Histories of Northern Animals* (1909), *Birds of Manitoba* (1891), *Mammals of Manitoba* (1886), and countless magazine articles on wildlife. He was commissioned to illustrate the *Century Dictionary*'s animal and bird sections as official

The artist sketched the home of John Duff, a family friend, while still an art student in Canada.

Duffs House.

Lone Spruce Hill on horizon at left

naturalist for the **Province of Manit**oba. As his sketch pad grew in size, he wrote and illustrated a collection of books on small game and birds: _Wild Animal Play for Children_ (1900), _Pictures of Wild Animals_ (1901), _Woodmyth and Fable_ (1905), _Animal Heroes_ (1905), _Natural History of the Ten Commandments_ (1907), _The Biography of a Silver-Fox_ (1909), _Wild Animals at Home_ (1913), _The Preacher of Cedar Mountain_ (1917), _Woodland Tales_ (1921), _Bannertail_ (1922), _Cute Coyote and Other Animal Stories_ (1930), _Bingo and the Racing Mustang_ (1930), _Billy, the Dog that Made Good_ (1930), _Famous Animal Stories_ (1932), _Biography of an Arctic Fox_ (1937), _Great Historic Animals_ (1937), and _Santana, the Hero Dog of France_ (1945).

Seton's preoccupation with big-game animals dates back to his early sketching days as an art student in London, where he did many drawings of such animals as lions, tigers, and wolves in the London zoo. But it was not until he lived on the plains of Manitoba as a man in his twenties that he began any serious attempt to draw big game in the wild. His first efforts were directed toward sketching and painting wolves, coyotes, deer, and moose. In later life—especially after making trips to the Pacific Northwest and the Rocky Mountain area—much of his art featured buffalo, antelope, elk, and the large bears.

The passing of the buffalo and the animal itself fascinated him as much as wolves and the Indian did. His personal totem—dating from his early days with the Woodcraft League and his Camp Fire Club days—incorporated the buffalo horns. Out of his studies of the big bears came his books _Biography of a Grizzly_ (1900) and _Wild Animals I Have Known_ (1898). _Krag and Johnny Bear_ (1902) was inspired by his research into the Rocky Mountain bighorn sheep, and his character Lobo will remain an American outdoor classic of wolf writing. His studies of Rocky Mountain mule deer and elk led him to write _Trail of the Sandhill Stag_ (1899). _Monarch, the Big Bear of Tallac_ (1904) grew out of another encounter with a cattle-killing grizzly.

Lives of the Hunted (1901), _Wild Animal Ways_ (1916), and _Mainly About Wolves_ (1937) were mostly concerned with big-game animals. But Seton's monumental work on big game was his four-volume _Lives of Game Animals_ (1925–27), for which he was awarded the John Burroughs Medal in 1926.

Young Seton had already done some good work and had received considerable encouragement from art teachers at the Toronto Collegiate Institute and the Ontario School of Art—particularly from Mrs. C. M. B. Schreiber, who was responsible for Ernest's winning the Gold Medal in art for the winter term of 1878–79. On the morning of June 12, 1879, Ernest stood on the deck of the _Algerian_ in Toronto harbor, bound for Montreal and England. He arrived in London on August 28, 1879, took a small bedroom at 66 Albany Street, and set about attempting to get into the Royal Academy of Art. The entrance examination was competitive. His first drawing of _Hermes_ was submitted and rejected. His second entry, a painstaking drawing of Michelangelo's _Satyr_, was sent in a year later, and in December 1880 Seton—out of hundreds of applicants—was awarded a seven-year scholarship at the Royal Academy School of Painting and Sculpture. One of the fringe benefits of the scholarship was free admission to the huge London zoo, where he spent hours sketching and painting.

Many of Seton's animal paintings are superimposed upon excellent landscape work—sometimes missed by the casual observer. His painting of the female goat defending her young on page 26 is a fine example of this. The background is an English landscape done while Seton attended art school, and the red fox and goats were added years later. Of the landscapes and still-life paintings shown here, some have no wildlife in them—while others may have only a small bird or animal hidden away in the foliage. Although Seton never did much with sculpture, he did experiment occasionally. The bronze chowder-pot (still on the huge mantel over the fireplace at the Camp Fire Club, in Chappaqua, New York) is perhaps the most famous conversation piece because tradition has it that Dan Beard was associated with the decision to cast this pot. Other random pieces of sculpture are to be seen in his Santa Fe home and in the Seton Museum.

His knowledge of human anatomy served him well in his sketches of trappers, mountain men, cowboys, guides, and Indians in his many illustrations for books.

Few artists outside the pure sciences—such as zoology and ornithology—have attained so high a level of excellence in anatomy as Seton. His *Studies in the Art Anatomy of Animals* (1896) could stand today as a textbook for veterinarian medicine. The illustrations are marvels of study and work. It is no wonder that Seton's hasty sketches of animals and birds in the field were such works of art when one realizes the depth of his knowledge of anatomy. Passion for detail and burning curiosity to find out what role the intricate parts of animals and birds played in life and motion ran throughout his work for his entire life. A simple entry on October 30, 1882, speaks eloquently of Seton's scientific dedication.

I made a careful count of the feathers on a Brewer's grackle:

Head		*2226*
Back of neck		*285*
Front of neck		*300*
All below		*1000*
Back		*300*
Each thigh	*100*	*200*
Each wing	*280*	*560*
Flight feathers		*44*
		4915

Seton was fourteen years old when in the winter of 1874 he began building a cabin—a tiny wood shack—along a clear stream in a heavily wooded area on the outskirts of Toronto. It was the beginning of his lifelong devotion to woodcraft. The fact that it was wrecked by some card-playing, drunken tramps did little to dampen his enthusiasm for camping and the outdoors, and until his death in New Mexico at age eighty-six he was an expert in the field.

Seton may well have been the founder of the Boy Scout movement in America—although there has been considerable controversy and speculation about this. Both he and Dan Beard, at one time close friends and associates, claimed to have "invented" the scouting movement. Lord Baden-Powell of England is generally given credit for founding the Scouts. There is no doubt he founded the Scout movement in England along military lines, but Seton started an organization he called the Woodcraft Indians in 1902, wrote a manual for the organization, and later corresponded with Baden-Powell concerning the formation of the Scouts. This correspondence is available to students of Seton, Baden-Powell, the Scout movement, and Daniel Carter Beard, and it does indicate that Baden-Powell derived his program from Seton's Woodcraft Indians. Beard and Seton were co-founders and officers of the Boy Scouts of America, although later Seton was to disassociate himself from the organization in anger. In a magazine story about his formation of the Woodcraft Indians which appeared in the *Ladies' Home Journal* of May 1902, he pretty much substantiates his claim to be the originator of the movement in this country.

His experience with the Scout movement led Seton to write a great many books on woodcraft—much of which he patterned after Indian lore. His fascination with and admiration for things Indian encouraged him to write and illustrate many books on the subject. His two woodcraft books, *Two Little Savages* (1903) and *Rolf in the Woods* (1911), have been children's outdoor classics for half a century. In addition, he illustrated and wrote *American Woodcraft for Boys* (1902); *The Birchbark Roll* (1906); *Scouting for Boys* (1910); *The Arctic Prairies* (1911), a record of his incredible seven-month canoe trip to the Arctic and down Canadian rivers; *Forester's Manual* (1911); *The Book of Woodcraft and Indian Lore* (1912); *Manual of Woodcraft Indians* (1915); *The Woodcraft Manual for Boys* and *The Woodcraft Manual for Girls* (1916); and *Sign Talk* (1918).

JOHN G. SAMSON, NEW YORK, 1976

The bits and pieces that come down through the years are the things that a boy remembers—of Toronto in 1870 and the small settlement of Lindsay just to the northeast of the city.

There was the plain, practical two-story brick house built for the entire family and the odors of new wood—lime from the masonry work and the dank chill of new rooms. The chill grew deeper as winter came on hard, drifting snow piled against the brick walls, the days rang with the sounds of axes and the air carried the acrid smell of woodsmoke from the chimneys.

Even a seven-year-old could vividly remember the lessons taught by older brothers in those cold and far-gone days. It was a natural task for a small boy to hold the ends of planks which were being sawed—feeling the vibrations travel up through small wrists and slim arms as the pile of sawdust grew on the new floor and a brother's voice rang out.

"No, don't press down. That will break it off and leave a long splinter—maybe split both pieces!"

Other things a boy remembers: to turn a heavy grindstone wheel, ever so slowly, until the creaking sound threatens to put one to sleep—and a brother sharpens an ax on the wearying wheel, pushing against the direction of the turning and wetting the blade to keep the temperature down; setting nails in wood at random rather than in a straight line—which will split wood along the grain; window glass held under water can be cut by a pair of strong scissors.

A boy could be expected to remember—even at this tender age—how molten lead jiggled in the heating pot and slithered quickly into bullet molds—and molds for anchors, wheels, and ship keels. A brittle-cut nail may be softened by fire and slow cooling—so that later it can be bent and inched like wrought iron. And all handy youngsters were taught to use a rip and cross-cut saw and to know the uses and differences between awl and scratch-awl, plane and jack-plane, hewing ax and splitting ax. A boy was expected to understand the curve of an ax handle and that the only really satisfactory wood to make a helve with is white hickory wood of sapling growth—scraped to a fine finish with a piece of broken glass.

A lad could make a sliver-broom from blue beech, by cutting eighteen-inch slivers near one end and then bending them and binding them back beyond that end—or recall the mystery of bending wood for an ox-yoke by boiling it. And what boy today knows how to make a bull-toggle, a wooden clamp for a bull's nose, by boiling hickory so that it bends like lead, then drying it until it sets like iron? When a boy was eight or nine years old on the prairie provinces he knew that basswood was easy to cut and split but worthless as timber and poor as fuel. Beech and maple were the best firewood—hickory was too scarce for firewood, even in those days. Cedar wood was the best as shaving to start fires and made the finest shingles, but was no good when strength was needed.

It was common knowledge among boys that hickory is the strongest wood in the forest but rots in three years if set in the ground; hemlock knots are the hardest things that grow and can dull the blade of the sharpest ax; the crystal-clear sap from the dark bladder of a balsam tree is the best medicine for a bleeding cut; basswood is the best from which to carve whistles.

Youngsters of that day did chores around a country home or farm as a matter of course. Feeding chickens and swine and milking cows was as much a part of the days as early rising for school. Caring for livestock fell to boys, mostly, and sheep washing and shearing became second nature. There were tricks known to boys about livestock that were passed on from one generation to another—such as how to keep sheep from jumping fences either to escape or to raid vegetable gardens, or how to tie the two ears of the lead ram of a flock together—by piercing a hole in each of his ears near the tip. The first time he starts to jump a fence with his ears tied he will start, falter, and abandon the effort. Why? Every youngster knew that a sheep's ears must point forward as he leaps. And the memories of spring were strong in youth—the smell of the basswood buds and the tamarack shoots that were good to eat. There was the pleasant job of collecting hens' eggs—something that gratifies the hunter instinct. And nesting boxes for swallows and wrens were something to keep the hands busy—for childhood is a dreamworld where the hands must always be busy—anything to take part in the wild.

It takes years to know what a boy who loves nature knows instinctively—that nature is within us, if we have the eagerness to pursue it.

Not more than a quarter of a mile from the town house was the Don Valley, a land of open meadows and fascinating swamps—vocal with the meadowlarks, the bobolinks, flickers, and the winding river ripe with ducks, geese, and kingfishers. To the south of the city were the marshes and sand bars of Toronto Bay—filled with the wonder of shorebirds and the marshes alive with muskrats, mink, and the occasional otter.

The joy of a private zoo of captured wild things is indescribable. There were baby birds fallen from nests, an owl shot by a waterfowl hunter that recovered from its broken wing to make an exciting pet, turtles, frogs, snakes, salamanders, young crows, a baby raccoon, a red squirrel, and a young green heron—all cached in the garage and a source of joy each action-filled day.

But there was also the agony of not knowing so many things. The only book available on wild things was a copy of *Knight's Pictorial Museum of Animated Nature*—a two-volume book with plates and copy to match, but such a feeling of failure and loss! The animals and birds were all foreign—mostly European—and the books were no help in trying to identify Canadian birds and animals. Even so there were enough local names to suffice for most living things, and the days were filled with fishing and prowling the woods and swamps. There were plenty of perch, sunfish, and catfish in the shallow waters of the marsh, but the true joy was the riot of bird life. The reeds were filled with the rusty-gate squeak of red-winged blackbirds, with long-billed marsh wrens, robins, phoebes, barn swallows, sand martins, shore larks, twenty or so species of ducks, and at least four species of geese in the spring and fall. Both the bald and golden eagles were quite common near Toronto in those days. Ross' *Birds of Canada* cost the king's ransom of a dollar in 1875 and it took literally months of cutting and carrying stovewood, selling all a boy's marbles and dime novels to raise that much money in a time when the pay for a fulltime house carpenter was twenty-five cents for a ten-hour day. The day came when a fifteen-year-old walked into Piddington's Book Store and asked for the treasured book. Expecting the proprietor to say all copies had been sold, the boy was stunned to hear him ask casually, "Green or brown cover?"

"Green!" was the gasping reply, and the way home was spent trying to walk and absorb all the plates and reading material at the same time. Only later, in the following few years as the knowledge grew about the birds, would the realization dawn of the book's vast inadequacies—unanswered questions, missing species, and incorrectly classified birds. In 1882—even armed with a copy of Coues' *Key to North American Birds,* an art education from the Royal Academy of Art in London, and Jordan's *Manual of Vertebrates,* a twenty-two-year-old youth was under a considerable handicap in discovering,

classifying, sketching, painting, and writing about the complete animal and bird world of Canada. But since youth has the good fortune not to know of its inabilities, a young man boarded a train in Toronto on March 16, 1882, and headed west to the vast central Canadian province of Manitoba, more than a thousand miles from native haunts of Toronto. Two brothers, Arthur and Charlie, were living in a "claim shanty" near the small town of Carberry, about 100 miles west of the city of Winnipeg—building a frame house and preparing to look for more farmland. A friend, Bill Brodie, twenty dollars in cash, and thirty dollars' worth of poultry made up the rest of the entourage. Fifteen days later—after several days trapped in a blizzard, the train arrived at Winnipeg. In a few days the youths found the two brothers holed up in the rough, one-room log-and-sod shanty, with only the stovepipe sticking out of a mound of snow—and so began the truly creative years.

As the last of April and the beginning of May flooded across the huge prairie province, the entire world came alive after the deep freeze of winter snow and ice. Ice-cold streams flooded their banks and the land was awash with sinks, water-filled potholes, and ponds. On the great plains of the Souris tens of thousands of birds suddenly appeared from the south—flock after flock, reaching to the horizon. There were lap longspurs, flocks of brown cranes, and occasionally pairs of whooping cranes, trumpeting in the sky or seen on a prairie ridge bowing and dancing in the spring ritual mating dance.

And overhead came the V's of geese—snows, Canada geese, Ross' geese, the white-fronted and the blue geese—winging ever north, filling the skies with their cries. Then there were the flocks of swans, the trumpeters and whistling swans, necks stretched and wings set as they glided into the prairie sloughs to feed before continuing the voyage. Along the river valley were scattered oaks, and in old woodpecker holes were flocks of

purple martins nesting the way they had for millions of years before man thought of building martin houses. On an alkali flat north of the Pembina Valley a willet flew from its nest—leaving four triangular eggs, points in, to make a circle divided into equal parts.

The verdant prairie suddenly sprang alive with all forms of rodent life—gophers, mice, Richardson's and Franklin's ground squirrels, rabbits—and with them came the predators, the prairie foxes, coyotes, wolves, and the hawks and eagles. Tree limbs were studded with the big buteo hawks—the Swainson's, the red-tailed, and rough-legged hawks. The tiny sparrow hawks hovered, fixed in the sky, their tapered wings beating rapidly as they waited for a mouse or chipmunk to show itself. The accipiters—the big goshawks, the smaller Cooper's hawks and the smallest sharp-shinned hawks—whipped through the tree limbs and brush in pursuit of the migrating hordes of birds, zooming silently with their prey from close to the ground to a limb near the trunk of a tree. And overhead an occasional turkey vulture performed lazy circles in the sky—its wings seldom beating as it rode the warming currents of air.

Badgers and skunks lurked in the sprouting prairie grass—both seeking rodents and eggs of nesting birds. Ducks by the thousands flew overhead and skittered across the surface of the prairie impoundments—the puddle ducks jumping from each grassy slough as they were disturbed. The snipe were everywhere, as were meadowlarks—their trilling warble announcing to all the full glory of spring. Vesper sparrows ran mouselike ahead of a walking man, and blackbirds, bronze grackles, and Brewer's blackbirds swarmed over the stubble grain fields. Swarms of crows and ravens made the sky noisy with their calls. All were noted down and the dates entered in the journals. Each bird collected with the shotgun was carefully sketched and then as carefully dissected to learn its stomach content and to draw its

---

The English countryside landscape was painted by the artist when he was an art student in London. Many years later he needed a setting for his painting of a red fox threatening a domestic nanny and her kids and simply superimposed the animals upon the landscape.

anatomy. Days sped by in an agony of fulfillment—yet with the knowledge that there was so much unknown and being left undone. The sheer joy of life coursed through young veins, and one could run across the prairie—splashing through shallow water and leaping small streams like any other wild creature—with head thrown back and a laughter carried by the spring wind.

The swarms of ducks and killdeer, the strings of geese and flocks of prairie chickens alighted on the stubble grain fields, and the forests abounded with arriving hordes of towhees, whippoorwills, flycatchers, woodpeckers, and the warblers—warblers by the thousands in a myriad of colors. As each day sped to its end, the notebook became crammed with drawings and notations, to be carefully packed away and a new, crisp one taken out. A flicker nest was found on May 31, the yolk plainly visible through the translucent white of the shell.

And mixed with it all spread the glory of the sandflower, or the pasqueflower, covering the sandy ridges with its layer of lilac snow as far as the horizon. On the prairies all across the Canadian provinces, southward into the Dakotas, and westward to the Rockies, the magnificent sandflower burst into bloom and the many living things—buffalo, horses, cattle, deer, cranes, geese, prairie chickens, and the millions of rodents—all fattened themselves on this feast of budding stems. Many other plants follow the death of the sandflower on the prairies, but there is little to equal the silent burst of color as a world awakens from the long winter sleep. The sandflower is followed by the prairie daisies, the yarrow, the harebell, the sunflower, and the flame of lilies.

In June came the prairie rose, its wealth of color followed by the growth of rose hips hanging on branches which, though filled with thorns will provide life for wild things after the snows have come again. The goldenrods follow and remain until the fall nips them to

sleep, but it is the sandflower one remembers longest.

With the summer came the torture of the mosquitoes—the curse of cattle, wild things, and men since the beginning in these northern latitudes. Man could get behind the smudges, built in three-foot-wide and one-foot-deep trenches. A good fire of dry wood was laid in the trench and then covered with damp straw or a layer of sod. Heavy black smoke poured out for hours, rolling downwind and staying close to the ground in the evening air. The smudges were lit every night from May to September. Insect-crazed cattle would gallop downwind of them to stand in the blessed fumes. As the smudge would shift with the wind so would the lines of cattle, striving to stay within the pall of acrid smoke.

And the fall months passed, with the birds returning south and the plains animals gradually retreating southward until the first snows drove them away or underground. The many owls followed them south—leaving a few great-horned predators to prey on the snowshoe hares and ruffed grouse and the big snowy owls to prey on anything smaller than themselves.

In the morning, when there should have been daylight, it was still dark with the chaos of whirling snow. In the blizzards, visibility is limited to less than twenty feet and racing clouds sweep close to the earth. Wind screams around a house or dugout shanty—finally turning into a deafening roar—as though a speeding freight train was steadily passing a few yards away. It seems impossible that any life could exist in such an environment, but there is a tiny bird, the snow bunting, which seems perfectly at home in the frozen world. Burrowing into the snowbanks at night as the temperature drops and blizzards shriek, they drift south before the ferocity of winter. The tiny members of the finch family appear like snowflakes themselves as they feed merrily ahead of a storm. Their calls, sounding like a tinkling whistle, carry across the frozen and barren ground as they feed on almost in-

These field sketches, crude and in a notebook, were made with instantaneous recognition features in mind. Seton later refined these to include both flying birds and on-water birds. His was the first such system and was later adapted by great ornithologists such as Roger Tory Peterson.

Meadowlark

White Crane

Whistler

Black Duck

Old Squaw

Snipe

Marsh Hawk

Bp. Gull

Pintail Gr.

Nighthawk

T. Buzzard

Ruffed Gr.

 visible food such as pigweed, ragweed seeds, and the seeds of tiny grasses.

But the blizzards and the snowbirds and the great white owls are all to be replaced by another spring and the cycle begins again. The collection of study-skins increases—sparrow skins of the white-crown, chewink, song sparrow, and the white-throat.

With the English naturalist R. Miller Christy, there were the magnificent field trips around the Chaska-Water, the body of water named for the Indian friend Chaska. To the west and north the sandhills housed spruce and aspen stands—the special haunts of grouse, foxes, wolves, badgers, martens, fishers, mink, raccoons, and the deer, elk, and moose. To hunt the bounding black-tail deer and the moose brought a pounding of excitement to the temples and a dampness to the palms. The days were filled with skinning and dissecting and the notes, notes, notes on each and every detail.

And later it was ever farther into the Arctic, where the woodland caribou and the woods buffalo dwelt, and where the wolverine, the great wolves, and the tufted-eared lynx stalked their quarry on the barren and rock-studded tundra. The wonder of the musk ox was in no way dimmed by the incredible sight of barren-ground caribou herds stretching to the horizon.

From Great Slave Lake to Artillery Lake and finally to Aylmer Lake close to the Arctic Circle, and return—a six-month canoe trip of 2,000 miles brought the North home as no other way. The land of the white owl and the lemming, the slovenly Chipewyan Indians, and the starving dogs—this land of lichens and bugle moss remains forever. Beaver dams and the horror of black flies; lynx sighted on the banks as canoes floated past, and a world of fragile cranberry, crowberry, and cloudberry on a lichen-covered landscape. . . . JOHN G. SAMSON

The details of the pine and pine cones are almost as precise as Seton's exacting treatment of the crossbills.

Prairie Chicken, Killdeer, Passenger Pigeons, Upland Plover, Pintail, Kingbird, Snowbird, White-Throated Sparrow, Western Meadowlark, Bittern, Green-Winged Teal, Prairie Horned Lark, Veery, Brown Bear, Elk, Deer, Polar Bear, Sharpshin Hawk, Caribou, Buffalo, Moose, Musk Ox, Red Fox, Kit Fox, Wolf, Wolverine, Canada Lynx, Rabbits & Lynxes, Chipmunk, Marten, Dog, Fisher, Ground Squirrel, Sea Otter, Porcupine

Prairie Chicken

Throughout May and June I found the chicken dance taking place; and later I learned that even in the autumn, when feeling fat and fit, they assemble at the Dance Hill on fine days for a spiel. But a more remarkable demonstration was in store for me.

In the summer of 1883, at Carberry, Manitoba, I had some fifteen baby prairie chickens hatched under a hen. When they were two weeks old, we were visited by a cold driving storm of sleet. The chicks were in danger of perishing.

I brought the whole brood into the kitchen. Keeping the hen in a cage close by, I put the chilled and cowering little things under the stove, on the tin which protected the floor. Here, after half an hour, they were fully warmed. They recovered quickly, fluffed out their feathers, preened their wings, and began to look very perky. . . .

It seemed to stir them with some new thought and feeling of joy. One of the tiny things, no bigger than a sparrow, lowered his head nearly to the tin, with beak out level, raised high the little pimple where in time his tail should be, spread out at each side his tiny wings; then ran across the tin, crowing a little bubbling crow, beating his wings, and stamping with his two pink feet so rapidly that it sounded like a small kettledrum.

The result was electrical. At once the rest of them leaped up and at it. Every one took the same position—head low, wings out, beating, tail-stump raised and violently vibrated, the feet pounding hard—leaping, bounding, stamping, exactly as is done by the old birds on the Dance Hill at love time.

For a minute or more it lasted; then they seemed tired, and all sat down for a rest.

In half an hour they were at it again; and did it several times that day, especially when the sun was on them, and they were warm and fed.

Then I found that I could start them, when the conditions were right, by rattling on the tin a tattoo with two fingers. They responded almost invariably; during the three days that I had them in the house, I started them dancing many times for myself or the neighborhood to see. A number of my friends made a buggy drive across country those days to come and see the tiny downlings "do their war dance," whenever I chose to start them by beating the drum.

It is noteworthy that these chickens danced exactly as their parents do, without ever having seen those parents; therefore, the performance was wholly instinctive. All—and undoubtedly both sexes were represented—danced with equal spirit. It was not at the breeding season, and could not, in any sense, be said to have a sex urge. It was evidently and unquestionably nothing more nor less than a true dance—a vigorous, rhythmic, athletic expression of health and joy.

TRAIL OF AN ARTIST-NATURALIST, 1940

Killdeer

July 2. We arrived at Fort Ellice. As we drove the striding oxen, a killdeer appeared overhead, swooping at us and screaming in anger. Then, on the road before us, I saw the cause of her anxiety. Running in the deep rut of the trail, unable to get out, was a new-hatched baby killdeer. It could not escape; the oxen were almost upon it. So I leaped out, ran ahead and caught it in my hand.

It was a tiny ball of down, marked in colors much as are the parents, except that the orange on the rump was lacking. It had large brown liquid eyes, and looked up at me quite fearlessly, while its parents screamed overhead.

I thought it the tenderest, sweetest wee thing I had ever seen in feathers, a veritable fawn in tiniest miniature. Its shining eyes beamed with kindly confidence. I set it down at a safe place to one side, where its frantic parents speedily found and repossessed it.

How is it that all birds of the lower orders are beautiful at birth, and all of the superior groups are as ugly as can be?

TRAIL OF AN ARTIST-NATURALIST, 1940

Flocking and Flight Habits

During the fall and winter of 1881, when associated with Bill Loane, Bill Lang, Sam Humphreys, and other gunners of Toronto Bay, I had been much struck by the remarkable way in which these men could identify their game, even when it was flying a quarter mile off.

When I exclaimed: "How do you do it?" their unsatisfactory answer usually was, "Practice."

I soon observed, however, that the first essential is to know what species are to be expected at a particular season in a particular region and environment.

The second is to know their habits of flocking and flight. Thus, the geese and cranes fly high, in long lines, or sometimes in V-shape; the canvasbacks and some waders fly in lines, but keep low. The teals, stints and blackbirds, as well as all small birds, fly in irregular flocks. Briefly, all large birds that fly in flocks adhere to the line or V-formation. Orderly flight is apparently a question of size; evidently a collision would be more serious to the larger birds.

Recently several of my friends in the aviation service have told me that, when flying in squadron formation, the airplanes copy the wild geese. When so marshalled, each airplane is behind the leader; and yet every pilot has a clear view of him, as well as of the course ahead. If one plane should, by accident, fall back, there is no danger of collision. And, finally, none of them are flying in "churned air." Just so, the geese.

The last secret of the gunners is to know the recognition marks, which render service as the birds come into much nearer view. Every species has its own peculiar labels.

These marks, or labels, I set to work to learn and map down on paper. I then called them "flying descriptions," "far views," or "far portraits." On the Plains in 1882, and in subsequent years, I drew hundreds of these impressions which, chiefly, are the fieldman's far-off identification.

In the *Auk* for October, 1897, pages 395–96, I published a paper on the subject, calling it "The Directive Coloration of

No detail was too insignificant for the artist—such as the exact number of primary and secondary flight feathers.

Birds," giving the underside marks of twelve hawks and six owls. The same plate, with new text, I published in *Bird Lore,* November, 1901, pages 187–88, under caption "The Recognition Marks of Birds." In *Two Little Savages,* 1903, I gave two plates of these "Far Portraits" of ducks. My journal contains scores that have not yet been published. My first studies and sketches of the subject were made during those tramps in Toronto Marsh in 1881. The first methodical approach, however, was made on that land hunt into the Pembina region in 1882.   TRAIL OF AN ARTIST-NATURALIST, 1940

Passenger Pigeons

In the present tolerant attitude of the family, I saw a chance to score—to secure some new legislation. I asked if I might have a gun "when I got well." As I was strongly backed by Mother, the paternal consent was given, though grudgingly; and I think helped by the doubt that I ever would get well. This is how it came about that, at the age of fifteen and one half, I was technically permitted to have a gun, provided I bought it myself.

In those days, the most conspicuous and abundant of the wild life about us was the huge flocks of wild pigeons that came over in spring and fall. All of my school friends reckoned on the pigeon shooting as the most thrilling of the wildwood pastimes. But, as already noted, the high command at home had before this excluded me from the sport.

But now, with the embargo removed, I began to intensify my interest in the pigeon flocks. I shall never forget the last great horde that passed over. It was in 1876, about April 20.

An army of pigeons flew overhead due north. The flocks seemed only about twenty deep, but extending east and west as far as could be seen, fading into a smoky line on each horizon. . . .   TRAIL OF AN ARTIST-NATURALIST, 1940

Upland Plover or Bartramian Sandpiper

As I look over the ancient record written by the campfire at night, I am conscious of this: that the detail of birds and beasts, with set and science names, as given in my paper record, is not the real thing.

This was the new light—spiritual joy, the lasting memories of life—life—beautiful life on every side. With this thought, I give the impress of a bird that dominated plains and sky.

"Quailie" is the name by which he was known to us in the early time; but nowadays the uncomprehending bookmen have renamed him "upland plover" or "Bartramian sandpiper." How can they expect such names to become part of the language of the wilds?

Early in the morning we heard his strong and vibrant whistling call from the upper sky, a whistling, wailing note like "*r r r r pheoo pheoo pheoo,*" and louder as he lowers, and now appears, sailing on wings set stiff but with points vibrating. Then down, down, with a long swift swoop, and the quailie is on the prairie, where for a moment he stands in rigid pose, with wings uplifted—up, straight up, like an angel's wings, displaying their undersides with their vivid checkering of black and white. For a few seconds he stands as though conscious of their beauty; then slowly folds them, to nod and run and forage in the grass, then raise his voice in the long quailie cry that conjures from the clouds his mate, his friends, his prairie clan, to sail to the broad flat sea of grass, then strike the angel pose, and join in the nodding run. This combination of a beautiful pattern and a deliberate, persistent effort to display it must be a compelling force in the evolution and perfecting of that pattern.

All day long, we heard that wailing cry, and saw the swift down-swoops, the angel pose. At this long later date, some sixty years after, the song comes back and the scene of the song, with power I do not find in later happenings that were of immensely greater moment to all the world about me.

TRAIL OF AN ARTIST-NATURALIST, 1940

This unfinished watercolor of the English turtle dove is believed to have been painted in a Canadian zoo.

Australian Duck

mud duck.

Pintail

Doubtless many older readers will know that the pintail is a common kind of wild-duck, and they may also know that its name is derived from the long and pointed shape of its tail. Some are perhaps familiar with the bird itself as a museum specimen, but probably very few have had opportunities of seeing it undisturbed, and in its native haunts.

Those readers who are members of the Agassiz Association will have learned that no one can safely undertake to identify any strange bird or beast, without having it in hand to measure and to examine; but it must not therefore be forgotten that valuable knowledge may be acquired by watching the living creatures from a distance, by means of a telescope. The pintail standing stuffed in museums, and the pintail lying all mangled and bloody, were perfectly familiar to me, but it was long before I had any idea of the perfect gracefulness of the living bird. Nor was it until I began to use the telescope, as well as the gun, in making my researches, that my eyes were opened. And then I found that a new and a delightful field of study was before me, yet untouched. Ducks far distant on some pond were brought apparently within arm's length by the magic of the field glass; and shy birds, familiar, while living, only as far-away blots of black and white on the quiet water, now were seen to be graceful creatures, full of animation, quietly pursuing their ordinary way of life, seemingly by my very side.

Many times since have I thrown myself in the grass by some reedy lake, and delighted my eyes with such a scene as that suggested above. All the drawings, all the dead birds I had ever seen, and all the descriptions I had ever read, failed to give me any idea of the beauty and symmetry of this, the most elegant of all our ducks, the delicate arrangement of whose colors so added to the effect of the perfect form as to make the bird even more strikingly graceful than Queen Swan herself—whose form, indeed, is so closely copied by her smaller cousin with the lengthy train.

In my Manitoban home, I had many good chances to study

Attitudes, stances, and moods such as seen in these wildfowl drawings can come only from years of observation.

the pintail, and so great was my admiration for its appearance that I had determined to attempt to tame some for the barn-yard, and welcomed the opportunity at length afforded by finding a nest not far from the house. It was formed of marsh grass and feathers, and was placed under a willow bush, close to the water. The eggs, nine in number, I took home, and placed under a hen. In the course of a few days they were hatched, and the ducklings were at once given their liberty in company with their foster mother, whom they followed closely thenceforth, and thus learned quiet, domestic habits before their wild natures had an opportunity to develop. When hatched, they were clad in golden yellow down, spotted with black. . . .

Almost as soon as they were hatched they could leap out of a common waterbucket, so great was the length of their legs, even from the very first. They soon grew so large that the hen was kept standing all night in an attempt to cover them, and so tame they were a perfect nuisance about the house. But the intense satisfaction of seeing them thrive so well, amply repaid me for all the trouble incurred by the experiment.

Alas!—just as they were beginning to put on the swan-like beauty and adult feathers of their kind, some miserable thief broke into the henhouse and took them all in a single night. That was the end of my tame pintails, for I have not since had a fitting time to repeat the experiment.

I am satisfied, however, that it would be quite easy to add this graceful bird to our parks and ornamental waters, if not indeed to make it a common sight upon our farm ponds and in **our barn-yards everywhere.** ST. NICHOLAS MAGAZINE, SEPTEMBER, 1888

Kingbird

One of the earliest of my wild-life thrills was given by the kingbird. I had heard of the feathered monarch —his prowess, and the fact that, though little larger than a sparrow, he would assail and drive off any hawk—yes, even an eagle.

One day, as I went for the cows with my older brother George and a neighbor, Jim Parker, a couple of crows flew high across. Then, from a low tree, there launched out a small bird that uttered a shrill war cry; and dashed first at one, then another of the big black fellows. They dodged and swooped in evident fear, and flew as fast as possible into the woods.

"What is that?" I asked eagerly.

"That's a kingbird," said my brother, for he had been learning from the woodsmen.

"An' he kin lick anything that flies," was added by the neighbor.

"A kingbird!" I gasped. Yes, and gulped a cup of joy. I had dreamed of it. I thought it a rare bird of far countries. Now I had seen it in our own land, with my own eyes, it had all become real. It lived and fought right here among *our* crows. The fact was glorious, stunning, in its magnitude. That man never knew how much he was giving me.

TRAIL OF AN ARTIST-NATURALIST, 1940

Snowbird

The icy coating on each window pane grew thicker and denser as winter wore on. Nothing was visible through the glass. Nearly every day and all night the hiss and grinding of the blizzard wind showed us how wise were those birds that southward fled for winter, and those beasts that retreated far underground and slept away the long hard peril of the cold.

Yet there was one little bird that never once seemed to be afraid—the snowbird, the snowbunting. All winter he was seen about our barns, roosting in holes, burrowing deep into a snowbank when the feeble sun went down, and living on the waste of the stable—fed, warm and happy.

I wondered if they were the same individual snowbirds all winter. To decide this, I made a box trap and captured three or four each week; then, right in the center of their breasts, I painted, with black ink, a spot as big as a bean, and let them go.

My plan was to watch for these "spotters," and see if they continued about our barns. But I never saw them again, so I suspect that even the snowbirds were drifting south before the ferocity of winter and the blizzard wind.

TRAIL OF AN ARTIST-NATURALIST, 1940

The artist caught the Canada goose not only incubating eggs (upper left), but sleeping (on one foot) and asleep lying down.

1886" E. T. Seton

White-Throated Sparrow

During those days, the naturalist was strong in me, and the knowledge-hunger grew till it became a pain. For we had no guides; and no one but myself seemed to believe that these woodlore glints were the only worth-while things in life. Each summer, I heard the whistler, and tried to imitate the song. Then, one year, in April, the end of late maple-sugar time, a spring bird flew to a distant tree, and uttered the familiar song. For some reason it thrilled me then in the silent snowy woods far more than it did in the hot days of the berrying time.

Still no one had a name for it; it was merely a delightful mystery, a mystery so elusive that it made me sad.

This had been during the late '60s and early '70s. My interest in birds grew ever more intense. Through school books, I learned of Wilson and Audubon; later, of Nuttall, Baird and Burroughs. . . .

"It's a new bird," I told myself. "None of these men ever heard it. I shall describe it"; for by now I had learned that men described and named new birds, when such came to hand. "I shall call it the Canadian nightingale, or the singer in the pines. I shall seek out its Indian name, and teach the boys."

Into my life then came another sweeping change. This landed me in the far Northwest, made to know the birds; and equipped, for the first time, with a book—with nothing less than Coues' *Key*.

What a sunrise that was for me! No man can overestimate the blessing that that book has been to all the world of bird folk in America. Faults it had in abundance, I now know; but it was the first successful effort to take exact bird knowledge from the museum, and give it to the multitude, to place it within reach of all the world of those who loved to hold our birds, not as skins, but as living friends.

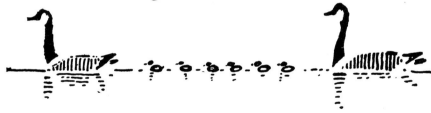

Under its inspiring force, my collection of bird skins grew; and about me there also sprang up a group of younger boys who, like myself, were keen to know the birds, but who had hitherto been wholly without guide.

Many sparrow skins did I collect—white-crown, chewink, song sparrow, whitethroat—male, female, and young. And still the soft whistler of the tamaracks was a mystery.

One of my bird friends said that he had traced this song to the singer, and it certainly was the hermit thrush. Another said he had seen it close, and it was the golden-crowned thrush. Yet another thought it was one of those rare birds found only in limited parts, and not yet known to science; while new descriptions of the song began to put the singer with the nightingale.

In those days I travelled much; and in 1882, was on the upper Assiniboine. In my journal for July 6, I find this note: "Shell River. This evening, our camp was on the edge of that yawning crack in the globe at the bottom of which runs the River Shell. As I walked along the edge, watching the setting of a red-hot sun that was sinking amidst clouds of purple fire, a small bird flew up from the gray woods, now in deep shadow, to the antlers of a dead tree, in full red glare of the sun, and stirred in me a hundred latent memories with a song that I have not heard for years. For a minute or so he sang; then dived down into the woods . . .

"This is a song I have been familiar with from childhood; but I have never seen the singer close at hand, and have found no one who could tell me its name. I am now satisfied that it is not, as I was told by one, the golden-crowned thrush.

"I could have shot the bird on this occasion, and so have gratified my longing to know, but a gentler feeling restrained my hand until it was too late."

Many times that summer, in the far elusive swamps, I heard the plaintive call. It still seemed to address me as a child: "Oh, yes, little one, little one, little one."

Then, on May 1, 1883, I was in Chicago with a day to put in. I wandered on to Lincoln Park. Here was a cage of common native birds. While I was yet some fifty feet away, I heard a note from one of the prisoners that gave me a prickling in my hair. The feeling that belongs to spring, or the spring itself, had stirred his genius of song. From that iron-bound cage there came the soft, sweet whistling of the swamp bird, my bird of the long ago.

I rushed forward to learn which had sung. There were sparrows of a dozen species, thrushes of three or four, chickadees, warblers, sora rails, and many more; but not a hint of which had sung. I waited an hour, but the song was not repeated. Then, dark as ever, I went on to my Assiniboine Land.

On May 12, 1883, I was out collecting birds near Carberry, Manitoba. It was a glorious day, and the skimpy fringe of woods by the slough was astir with birds. I had collected nearly as many as I could skin, when a gorgeous grosbeak flitted to a near-by tree, and called excitedly. I was intent on collecting him, when a hawk that looked like a broadwing sailed into another tree. I had but one shot left, and crept up quietly, hoping to secure a new hawk for my list. I was about to fire this, my last shot, when from a tree over my head, came a soft, sweet whistling that stirred a hundred memories. . .

Hawk and grosbeak were forgot. I had become somewhat hardened in the bloody business of collecting; but my hand trembled violently as I swung the gun around, aimed at the singer of the piping strain—and fired.

Down he came, stone-dead—a noble victim, sacrificed on the altar of the knowledge-hunger.

I rushed to the spot, to find that my sweet singer of the tamaracks, the whistler of the raspberry times, the night-singer of the Assiniboine, was neither more nor less than the white-throated sparrow, the Peabody bird of New England, the nightingale of the farther North.

With joy in my heart—and a tear in my eye—I laid the warm bloody little body in my basket.

TRAIL OF AN ARTIST-NATURALIST, 1940

Western Meadowlark

In the spring of 1882, I was sitting one day at the door of my house on the prairies of Manitoba, watching a furious thunder-storm, accompanied by a heavy rainfall. The rolling of the thunder was so incessant that the intervals between the peals rarely reached thirty seconds; but in such silent intervals as there were, I was surprised to hear again and again the sweet melody of the prairie-lark.

Eager to find the cheery bird, I took down my telescope, and from the door surveyed the plain, in the direction of the singing; and I at length discovered the brave little musician perched on a low twig, out in the storm. The rain was beating on his back and running in a steady stream from the end of his tail, but still he sang on, in the loud, melodious strains that have made the Western meadow-lark famous as a songster. He sat upon the bough so steadily, with one foot tucked up out of the wet, and sang with so little apparent intention of stopping on account of the weather, that I went for paper and pencil, and, observing him through the telescope, made a sketch which I afterward finished more carefully, and now present to the reader.

The other bird, on the wing, was added to show that the prairie meadow-lark also sings in the air, like a true lark.

It may be well to explain that the bird before us is very different from the common meadow-lark of the Eastern States. Though they are so much alike in appearance that none but an expert can distinguish them, they are so unlike in voice and habits that they need not be confounded by the young naturalist.

The song of the Eastern meadow-lark is a pleasing feature of the bird concerts in the fields of Eastern America; yet the song does not give the bird a position of superiority, nor even a place in the first rank of our songsters. But the song of the Western bird is loud, wild, melodious, and varied beyond description, and will yet secure for it the highest place of all in the estimation of those who delight in bird music.

ST. NICHOLAS MAGAZINE, NOVEMBER, 1888

The accipiters—the big goshawks, the smaller Cooper's hawks, and the smallest sharp-shin hawks—whipped through the tree limbs and brush in pursuit of the migrating hordes of birds zooming silently with their prey from close to the ground to a limb near the trunk of a tree . . .

Seton found the sharpshin hawk dead, rigged it up with wires, and created this marvelously lifelike flight painting from the model.

Lacking in movement and a little stiff, some of Seton's early paintings had a sort of precise Catesby quality about them—such as this male marsh hawk.

Bittern

From 1871 to 1879 the Marsh was my loved, ever-rewarding resort. Then came the London epoch of my life. My return to the Marsh in the fall of 1881 was important to me, and I began an exact study of its birds.

Perhaps the most remarkable of these was the dying-out species known as Cory's least bittern. This rare, and now extinct bird found its last strong-hold in Toronto Marsh. Most of the known specimens were taken there.

On July 30, 1885, after living four years in the Northwest, I paid a visit to Toronto Marsh with my old friend, Doctor William Brodie. The record in my journal gives some idea of the Marsh, its abounding life, and my mode of recording the same. We were especially in search of the Florida gallinule, water hen or mud hen, said to be rare north of Lake Erie.

"The sun arose just before we entered the Marsh, so that the birds had been feeding for some time before our approach. We rowed as cautiously as possible among the innumerable weedy openings which intersected the great rush bed; but all our attempts to surprise some swimmer on the open water seemed destined to fail. Yet the birds were quite numerous, and their interrupted croaks were heard in various directions, while now and again the prolonged laughlike calling fell upon our ears.

"Several times, on rounding some turn in the rush-hedged lanes, we saw on ahead a water hen with her half-dozen chicks, now nearly full grown, but they were generally out of range; and as we drew nearer, they swam away from the open water where they had been feeding on the *lemna* or duckweed, and gradually retired farther and farther into the rush beds as we approached. Usually when we were near, the old one, though out of sight herself, would croak at regular intervals, as though to let us know that she was quite close to the edge of the cover, and watching us; possibly these notes were meant also to warn the young ones, and keep them together.

"The retirement of the family, however, was not always as well timed; and after a number of unsuccessful approaches, we did succeed in getting within forty yards of a flock of the birds,

Bonaparte Gull
Dec. 1881. by E.T. Seton

Shore birds such as this Bonaparte gull abounded in the Toronto marsh, where Seton returned to sketch in 1881.

securing an old one; and a couple of the young almost immediately afterward. . . . Each time the gun was fired, it awoke a dozen near responses, loud and long, from as many water hens, who seemed unable to control their derisive laughter at the amusing harmlessness of an explosion evidently meant to injure them.

"Altogether during that morning in Toronto Marsh, we bagged five and saw about five times that number, of this commonly reported 'rare bird.'

"The young ones were of different ages, the youngest showing the largest proportionate development of the horn, spur, or claw on the alula.

"This was dissected afterward by Doctor Brodie and myself, and found to consist of a somewhat conical horny sheath or claw on a distinct phalanx, perfectly articulated to another, the two together forming a well-developed first digit.

"Doctor Brodie suggests that the claw assists the young bird in its passage through the grass, etc., much as in the hoatzin. I made a full-size drawing of this curious appendage. Professor Ramsay Wright of Toronto University doubted its existence at first; but on being shown said it was a discovery new to science." TRAIL OF AN ARTIST-NATURALIST, 1940

Green-Winged Teal

On July 5, 1882, at Silver Creek, Manitoba, I came across a female green-winged teal traveling with her brood of ten young ones across the prairie toward a large pool. The mother bird was in great grief on finding that she was discovered, but she would not fly away; she threw herself on the ground at my feet and beat with her wings as though quite unable to escape and tried her utmost to lead me away. . . .

This species, I think, unlike the bluewing, usually nests quite close to the water, so that it is probably owing to the drying up of the pond that this newly hatched brood found themselves forced to take an overland journey of considerable extent before they could find a sufficiency of water.

BIRDS OF MANITOBA, 1892

The swarms of duck and killdeer, the strings of geese and flocks of prairie chickens alighted on the stubble grain fields, and the forests abounded with arriving hordes of towhees, whippoorwills, flycatchers, woodpeckers, and warblers—warblers by the thousands in a myriad of colors . . .

A textbook-type painting of a bobwhite quail—with every feather in place.

Field-notebook sketches of a feeding quail and remarkably precise drawings of the head were probably, as in most of the artist's field sketches, done in a hurry.

Prairie Horned Lark

On May 12, 1882, at camp eight miles south of Brandon, midway between our tent and the fire ten feet away, I started a small bird from its nest. It ran away very reluctantly, and continued wistfully close at hand, running about among the tufts of grass in the glare of the fire, and returning each time as soon as it dared. At gray dawn I found her on the nest again; she slowly walked away when I approached to rekindle the fire, but returned almost immediately with her mate; and now, for the first time, I saw them plainly. They were a pair of shore larks. Encouraged, no doubt, by the presence of her mate, she once more crept up to her nest and took up her position on the eggs, although I was but five feet off. Frying our bacon over a brisk fire, I was very careful to avoid hurting the birds or their home; and breakfast being over, travelers, tent, fire, and horses all went off and left them to discharge their duties in peace. The nest contained three brown eggs; it was sunk in the ground, and was made of grass and fiber, and lined with two or three large feathers.

My first real acquaintance with the shore lark at his home was in Minnesota, in the last week in March, 1882. A fearful blizzard, of course, "the worst ever known in the country," had been raging for two days or more. On the third day, when it was nearly over, I was making my way out to see the cattle. All the fences and low buildings were buried in snow, but the tall form of an elevator loomed up out of a circle of bare ground, caused by the eddying of the blast, and here, in the very vortex of the storm, in the thickest of the fight, were three or four shore larks, bracing themselves against the driving wind and picking up the seeds that had been exposed by the displacement of the snow. Poor little things! I thought, you must be nearly at death's door; but even while I looked one of them, under the lee of the buildings, perched himself on a frozen clod and poured out his sweet, simple little song in a way that seemed to say, "How happy am I."

But the longest night will end; and it is not always winter, even at the Pole. The spring comes, and "the time of the singing birds" arrives, and the brown shore lark raises his horns with sprightly air, and those who may chance to see him are now reminded that he is a near kinsman to the famed skylark—that indeed he is a skylark. Thus far he has sung only while perching on some clod or stone, but now the ardor of his devotion to the demure little Quakeress by his side demands a more ambitious demonstration; so, ceasing to sing, he strenuously endeavors to associate with the white, piling cumuli, and having soared, apparently, near enough to be comfortably damp, while to us he appears a mere speck, he floats on vibrating wings, singing a song composed of a single note, oft repeated with lessening intervals; it may be suggested by the syllables *trick, trick, trick, trick, trick, trick, t-r-r-r-r-r-r-r,* the notes at last all running together like the drumming of a partridge. During this performance he has lost much of his altitude, but at once proceeds to regain it by a series of bounds before again repeating the song. This alternate soaring and singing is usually kept up for over ten minutes, then the musician, having exhausted his energy, suddenly stops and dashes down with one frightful headlong pitch, right into the grass. Upon going to the spot, one is surprised to find he has not been dashed to atoms by the violence of the fall, but springs up, uttering his usual call note, and flits further off, again to settle on the ground.

The whole performance will be seen to resemble very closely the serenade of the Missouri skylark, the chief difference being that the shore lark is inferior in music and staying powers, and also in that the latter remains more nearly over one particular place. Another point of dissimilarity is, the shore lark sings chiefly on the ground, while the skylark confines his effusions almost entirely to his moments of physical elevation.

The shore lark is the earliest of the prairie singers to begin in the morning, being even a little earlier than the meadow lark; it commences before there is any sign of dawn, and at night it continues until the plains are enveloped in perfect gloom.   BIRDS OF MANITOBA, 1891

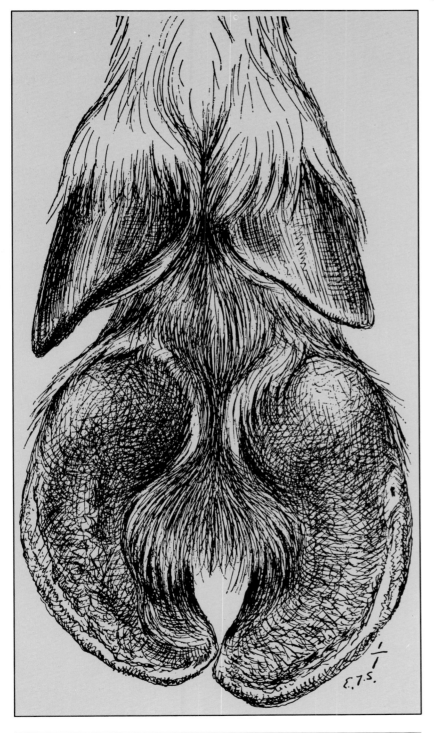

This illustration shows how the caribou can easily outdistance even the strong predators—such as the cougar and arctic wolf—by running on the soft, wet tundra footing. The hoof, including the dew claws, is almost a snowshoe—spreading wide upon impact.

Veery

On June 18, I heard a new arrival, yes, many of the species, singing a song that had been familiar for years in the low woods north of Toronto, but which I had never before identified. I attributed it to a thrush; some of my friends called it a wood thrush. But now, armed with Coues' *Key* and a telescope, I was able to jot down a full description of the performer. Yes, truly a thrush—all above tawny, all below white, marked with faint dusky spots. Beyond any doubt now, it was Wilson's thrush, the veery. The song was a soft but high-pitched whistle, rich and clear, with a rippling cadence as a brook. To render it in uncouth syllables seems vulgar, and yet it is most nearly suggested by the words "Veery Veery Veery," from which, no doubt, it gets the name by which the children **love** it.

But still from my early memories in Toronto days, because of his haunts in the low, thick alders and his rippling lay, he lives in my thoughts as the brook bird of the alder shades.

Flitting about among the new leafing poplar branches overhead was a new bird, evidently a flycatcher—very small, all above grayish olive, all below white with crissum slightly yellow; a white ring around each eye, two white wing bars, and each secondary edged white. His unceasing occupation is to flit about, catching insects, pumping his tail, and exclaiming *pichr se-wick* or *s-lick-split, plit* or *chebec,* according to your own interpretation. By these characteristics, I was able to identify it as the least flycatcher or chebec. . . .

In my journal for May, 1884, I find this: "Whoever would credit the chebec, a flycatcher, with singing a song? Yet today I saw one that, in the exuberance of his spring exhilaration, soared in the air above the bushes, and hovered in true flycatcher style to vociferate for half a minute a songlike '*chebec tooree-oorel; chebec tooree-oorel,*' etc., and having finished, gave a loud snap with his bill, a smack of delight, and sailed downward aslant into a bush where, no doubt, was perched the only spectator for whom the performance was meant, or whose opinion counted in the least." TRAIL OF AN ARTIST-NATURALIST, 1940

Each night the Coyote and the Fox came rustling about our camp, or the Weasel and Woodmouse scrambled over our sleeping forms. Each morning at gray dawn, gray Wiskajon and his mate [Canada jays]—always a pair—came wailing through the woods, to flirt about the camp and steal scraps of meat that needed not to be stolen, being theirs by right. Their small cousins, the Chicadees, came, too, at breakfast time, and in our daily travelling, Ruffed Grouse, Ravens, Pine Grosbeaks, Bohemian Chatterers, Hairy Woodpeckers, Shrikes, Tree-sparrows, Linnets, and Snowbirds enlivened the radiant sunlit scene.

One afternoon I heard a peculiar note, at first like the *"cheepy-teet-teet"* of the Pine Grosbeak, only louder and more broken, changing to the jingling of Blackbirds in spring, mixed with some Bluejay *"jay-jays,"* and a Robin-like whistle; then I saw that it came from a Northern Shrike on the bushes just ahead of us. It flew off much after the manner of the Summer Shrike, with flight not truly undulatory nor yet straight, but flapping half a dozen times—then a pause and repeat. He would dive along down near the ground, then up with a fine display of wings and tail to the next perch selected, there to repeat with fresh variations and shrieks, the same strange song, and often indeed sang it on the wind, until at last he crossed the river.

Sometimes we rode in the canoe, sometimes tramped along the easy shore. Once I came across a Great Horned Owl in the grass by the water. He had a fish over a foot long, and flew with difficulty when he bore it off. Another time I saw a Horned Owl mobbed by two Wiskajons. Spruce Partridge as well as the Ruffed species became common: one morning some of the former marched into camp at breakfast time. Rob called them "Chickens"; farther south they are called "Fool Hens," which is descriptive and helps to distinguish them from their neighbors—the "Sage Hens." Frequently now we heard the toy-trumpeting and the clack of the Pileated Woodpecker or Cock-of-the-Pines . . .

This painting of a wolf on a snowy prairie imparts the lonely, bitter-cold winter world of the great predator.

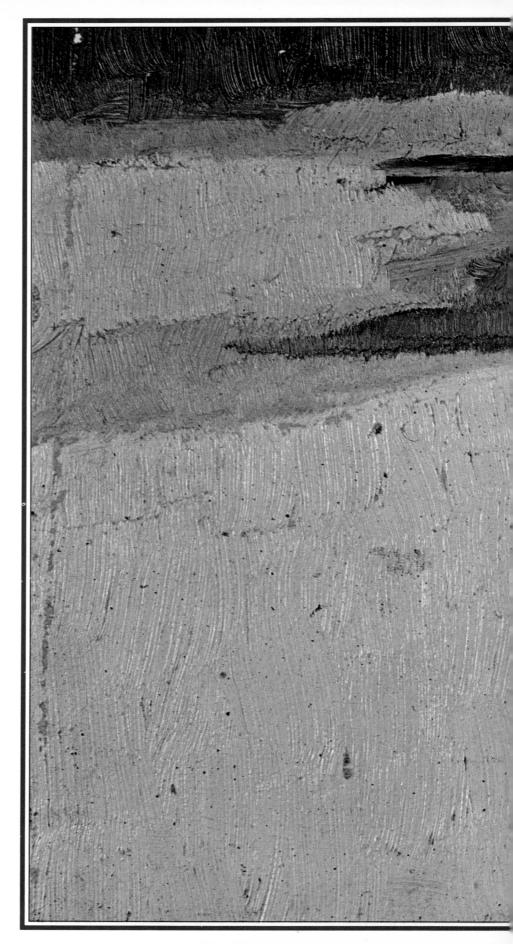

Ernest Thompson Seton

Mammals, too, abounded, but we saw their signs rather than themselves, for most are nocturnal. The Redsquirrels, so scarce last spring, were quite plentiful, and the beach at all soft places showed abundant trace of Weasels, Chipmunks, Foxes, Coyotes, Lynx, Wolves, Moose, Caribou, Deer. One Wolf track was of special interest. It was $5^1/2$ inches long and travelling with it was the track of a small Wolf; it vividly brought back the days of Lobo and Blanca, and I doubt not was another case of mates; we were evidently in the range of a giant Wolf who was travelling around with his wife. Another large Wolf track was lacking the two inner toes of the inner hind foot, the hind foot pads were so faint as to be lost at times . . .

All that night of Hallowe'en, a Partridge drummed near my untented couch on the balsam bough. What a glorious sound of woods and life triumphant it seemed; and why did he drum at night? Simply because he had more joy than the short fall day gave him time to express. He seemed to be beating our march of victory, for were we not in triumph coming home? The gray firstlight came through the trees and showed us lying each in his blanket, covered with leaves, like babes in the woods. The gray Jays came wailing through the gloom, a far-off Cock-of-the-Pines was trumpeting in the lovely, un-plagued autumn woods; it seemed as though all the very best things in the land were assembled and the bad things all left out, so that our final memories should have no evil shade.

The scene comes brightly back again, the sheltering fir-clad shore, the staunch canoe skimming the river's tranquil reach, the water smiling round her bow, as we push from this, the last of full five hundred camps.

The dawn fog lifts, the river sparkles in the sun, we round the last of a thousand headlands. The little frontier town of the Landing swings into view once more—what a metropolis it seems to us now!—The _Ann Seton_ lands at the spot where six months ago she had entered the water. . . .

I had held in my heart the wanderlust till it swept me away, and sent me afar on the back trail of the north wind; I have lived in the mighty boreal forest, with its Red-men, its Buffalo, its Moose, and its Wolves; I have seen the Great Lone Land with its endless plains and prairies that do not know the face of man or the crack of a rifle; I have been with its countless lakes that re-echo nothing but the wail and yodel of the Loons, or the mournful music of the Arctic Wolf. I have wandered on the plains of the Musk-ox, the home of the Snowbird and the Caribou. These were the things I had burned to do. _Was I content? Content!!_ Is a man ever content with a single sip of joy long-dreamed of?

Four years have gone since then. The wanderlust was not stifled any more than a fire is stifled by giving it air. I have taken into my heart a longing, given shape to an ancient instinct. Have I not found for myself a kingdom and become a part of it? My reason and my heart say, "Go back to see it all." Grant only this, that I gather again the same brave men that manned my frail canoe, and as sure as life and strength continue _I shall go._   ARCTIC PRAIRIES, 1911

Brown Bear

When one sees this mighty brute, this furry Elephant, marching like an unquestioned king in his bleak, fierce kingdom, it gives one a fearsome hint of those bygone days when first our race was nursed and builded up out of feebler stuff. It recalls those days of our paleolithic ancestors, when the huge Cave-bears, much the same as these, abounded; and the only weapons our people had were clubs or spears—when the Bear was king and man the underdog. The haunting fear of those awful days is gone, but has left its indelible imprint on our souls.

Something of this horror we find in the word "beast." Much of it we get in our terror of the moving shape at night, of the rustling leaf behind us in the gloom. But also among the memories inherited of those times, the joy we discover in the brightly blazing fire, instinct of those bygone days, when that fire meant safety and comfort.

The giant has become inoffensive now. He is shy, indeed, and seeks only to be let mind his own business. At the slightest hint of man in his vicinity, he will fly fast and far, and covers

While showing its massive form, Seton, somehow, managed to portray the bunched muscles and immense power of this great carnivore, the brown bear.

many mountains to be sure that he has left that dreaded taint behind. It is modern guns that has made this change of heart. Man with a club is one thing—a joke, an easy meal maybe. But man with a modern rifle is a very different creature. Irresistible is he, implacable, sure death. The Bear's one safety is in flight; he knows it; he has learned the lesson; he takes no chances. He flies.

A land of great plenty is this Alaska of the Bears. Foods of a thousand kinds are lavishly strewn, to be had for the gathering. So that when November comes with chilly nights, with ice-bound brooks, with hillside spreads of food no longer available, the Big Bear is fat; and, knowing when to quit, he seeks him out a den. Sometimes, it is a natural cavern in the rocks; sometimes under an upturned root. Sometimes it is a den dug in a bank-side by himself. But, wherever it be, it is always well drained, high and dry; and yet sure to be deeply buried in warm protecting snow, when the arctic blizzards hit their hardest.

A warm season may delay the den-up till November; it is largely a question of food. There have been one or two cases recorded of big he-Bears that did not den at all, but prowled the stormy shores the winter through. For the cold alone is nothing. Granting a sufficiency of food, he can blink his small eyes and square his great stern in total indifference, or even scorn, to the bleakest blizzard wind that ever blew.

LIVES OF GAME ANIMALS, 1925–1927

Elk

In 1882, when first I visited the Province, there **were** plenty of old antlers on the Carberry Sandhills. In the three years which followed I saw tracks three times, but once only did I see a Wapiti. This was a bull that was killed and brought to Carberry by some Indians in 1884. The head now hangs in the Western Hotel of that town. At that time the Wapiti was practically exterminated, except in the Pembina Hills and the Duck and Riding Mountains.

The dwindling process went on everywhere till about 1895. That was the low-ebb year in many parts of America for many kinds of game, but it was also the year of the great awakening. The lesson of the vanished Buffalo had sunk deep in men's minds. Thinking people everywhere recognized that unless the methods then practiced were stopped all our fine game animals would go the way of the Buffalo. They saw, too, that there was nothing to gain by extermination, and much to lose. Game protective societies, founded in various parts of America by men who viewed with hate the approaching desolation of the wilds, have now secured sound legislation for the protection of harmless wild animals, and public sentiment has secured a rigorous enforcement of these new laws. Thus in many regions the process of extermination has been stopped.

And not only has an end been put to extirpatory hunting, but the awakening has found its logical climax in serious efforts to re-stock many of the deserted ranges. Several areas whence the species had long disappeared have been re-peopled with Wapiti. Noteworthy among these are the Algonquin Park and the Adirondack Mountains Park. The former is in charge of Government officials, but the latter has been re-stocked chiefly through the efforts of a private "Society for Restoration of the Moose, the Wapiti, and the Beaver to the Adirondacks."

There is a widespread idea that the big bull is, as a matter of course, the leader of the Wapiti herd. This is not the case. It is well to remember how the animals get their leader. They certainly do not have any formal election, but they have instead a sort of natural election or process of elimination. This is the process: The individual in that band who can impress on the others that he is the *wise one*—the safe one to follow— eventually becomes the leader, and if there are any members of the band who do not wish to follow him, they have an obvious alternative—to go the other way. Thus the herd reaches unanimity.

Numberless observations show that this wise one is not the big bull, but almost invariably an *elderly female*. The big bull might drive them, but not lead them. She is the one that has impressed the others with the idea that she is safe to follow— that she will lead into no fool-traps; that she knows the best

This incomplete and badly stained watercolor painting nevertheless catches perfectly the pronghorn at rest. The keen eyes, however, betray the apparent lassitude.

pastures and the best ways to them; that she has learned the salt-licks, and the watering-places that are safe and open all around; that her eyes and ears are keen; and that she will take good care of herself and incidentally of the band. This female leadership is common to most, if not all, horned ruminants. One may ask, therefore, if it be not also a corollary of polygamy.

What becomes of these wonderful horns? Why is not the forest littered with them, since they are dropped and renewed each year?

First, the forest *is* littered with them to some extent in districts where the Elk abound. In several parts of the West I have seen small garden fences made of the cast-off antlers, and I am told that in California it was common to see a rotted survey stake replaced by a pile of Elk horns, which were the handiest and most abundant substitute. But still their numbers are nothing compared with what one might expect. If they were as durable as stones they would be as plentiful as stone in an ordinary Montana valley. The explanation is that they are easily destroyed by the elements . . .

The skull of the Elk may resist the weather for twenty years, the horns may crumble in half that time. As Caton long ago showed, while bone is one-third animal matter or gelatine, the antler substance is "about 39 parts animal matter and 61 parts earthy matter of the same kind and proportions as is found in common bone"; besides which the inner structure of the antler is exceedingly porous or cellular. "Soon ripe, soon rotten," is a North-of-England proverb that has a bearing on this case. **LIFE HISTORIES OF NORTHERN ANIMALS, 1909**

Deer Hunt

One day after we had become well acquainted, I went alone to the snowclad hills. Deer tracks led into the mixed forest at the eastward. Before following one of these, my attention was caught by a peculiar rubbing or scratching sound as of a deer scraping his horn on a branch, as they often do. I approached cautiously. I saw a small sapling shaking, and near its base, concealed by the brushwood, some

moving bulky animal. Aha! Now was my chance. I crawled up within forty yards and was about to fire when at the upper part of the creature I descried a bright red rag—and above it the jet-black hair of an Indian. I dropped the gun and cried in alarm, "Chaska!" Out he came; it was Chaska cutting some kinni-kinnik for his pipe. "Chaska," I gasped, "I nearly killed you. I thought it was a deer scraping his horns."

Chaska smiled and drew his finger across the red handker-chief that encircled his head and his ears. "We all wear that. Now you know why."

The differences in claws and profiles of three species of North American bears show clearly why the adult black bear is a tree climber and the other great bears are not.

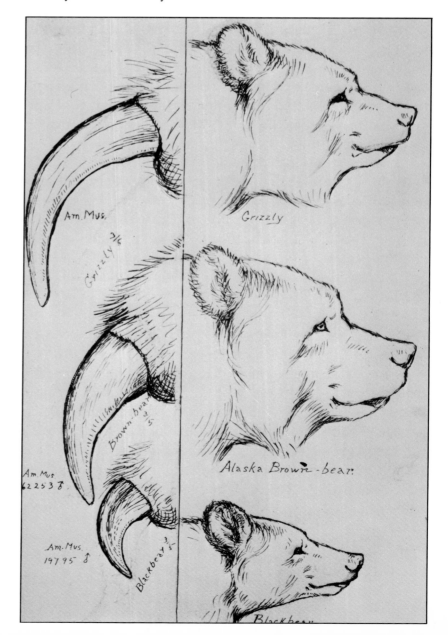

Late in the afternoon, as I guardedly peered over a rising, I caught a glimpse of what looked like a deer lying in the scrub beyond. I watched for a few moments until a slight movement of the ear dispelled all doubts. I tried in vain to get nearer; so having guessed the distance at a hundred and fifty yards, I put up the rifle. But oh! how terribly the muzzle wabbled, and I laid the weapon down with a groan—"it's no use."

After waiting a few minutes, I tried again, and finding my hand now steady fired. The deer jumped up, and stood looking about. I fired again and again; and then as he moved off, I wasted a fourth charge. My first shot went over, the second struck the center of his bed. The third and the fourth went wild. If the second had come first, I had won my deer; but as it was, he went off gaily bounding. I ran on the track for ten miles. While rapidly ascending a hill, I stumbled and had the misfortune to give my knee a severe blow on a projecting root. At night I reached home completely exhausted, after having travelled thirty miles on foot. TRAIL OF AN ARTIST-NATURALIST, 1940

Polar Bear

The great, long six-months day—the nightless day—is on the chilly islands of the Polar Sea. The day that dawned in mid-March to rule unbroken until mid-September is beaming on the cold, pale green expanse.

In the narrow strip 'twixt icy sea and icy cap that covers the uplands, are the bright, brave Arctic plants, making what hay they may in this, their little span of life. For now is springtime, heatherbell-time, and love-time.

There is much mystery about this romantic chapter of the White Bear's story. Lyon's Eskimo told him that May was Nahnook's merry month; others make it June. Hearne thought it as late as July or even August. The analogy of other Bears would make it late June. But so much is sure: it is in this long polar day, this season brief of flowers hedged round with ice, that Nahnook goes a-roaming—a-seeking for a mate.

But the Ice-king—what of his way? Is his appeal to eye, or ear, or nose, when the mating May-time thrills his world, and sends him gallivanting? Does he anoint the angle stones on the headlands with his body-scent? Does he gallop at random? Does he sing some loud, heroic song like a Lion roar? Or does he follow every trail that his discriminating nose announces as a she-Bear's trail?—till he finds her. And if it so be there arrive at that trail's end together two great King-bears of the ice, what then? A mortal combat, a finish fight, or a meek submission to the lady's judgment?

Of all this, we know nothing. It is recorded only that the mating is in midsummer. The Eskimo and Northern Indians say that this mating is a pairing. Polygamy has seemingly died out in the upper classes of the beasts.

LIVES OF GAME ANIMALS, 1925–1927

Sharpshin Hawk

In the September of that year (1876), I was prowling in the vicinity of my lost cabin, when, on the ground in a thicket, my eye caught sight of a dead hawk—a small one; but I got a full-sized thrill out of it. No doubt, some gunner had shot it and failed to find it. To me it was treasure trove. I carried it home, gloating over its beauty. I had had a few lessons in oil painting from a neighbor, an artist, Mrs. John B. McGurn; and set to work with enthusiasm to paint a portrait of my hawk.

After much experimentation, I devised a frame with clutches to hold the hawk in a flying position, and began my portrait. I did not know then, but learned afterward, that I had invented the very same apparatus as that which Audubon had used for his Bird Portraits.

I put in a couple of weeks painting my Sharpshin, for such it proved to be. Each dot and spot and streak was faithfully rendered, so that any one knowing the bird could identify it at a glance.

That picture is before me now. In the light of later knowledge, I should say that I dwelt too much on the detail and not enough on the larger forms. But still, it was a most conscientious portrait, and in all ways a forecast of my work and thoughts in the years that followed.

TRAIL OF AN ARTIST-NATURALIST, 1940

Caribou. Barrens
Ernest Thompson Seton

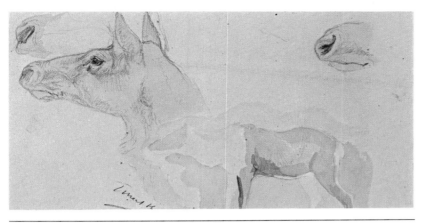

Caribou

A great many of the single Caribou I saw on my own Arctic journey were on the small islands. In 6 cases that came under close observation, the animals in question had a broken leg. A broken leg generally evidences recent inroads by hunters, but the nearest Indians were 200 miles to the south, and the nearest Eskimos 300 miles to the north. There was every reason to believe that we were the only human beings in that vast region, and certainly we had broken no legs. Every Caribou fired at (8) had been secured and used. There is only one dangerous large enemy common in this country, that is, the White Wolf. And the more I pondered it, the more it seemed sure that the Wolves had broken the Caribous' legs.

How? This is the history of each case: the Caribou is so much swifter than the Wolves that the latter have no chance in open chase; they therefore adopt the stratagem of a sneaking surround and a drive over the rocks or a precipice, where the Caribou, if not actually killed, is more or less disabled. In some cases only a leg is broken, and then the Caribou knows his only chance is to reach the water. Here his wonderful powers of swimming make him easily safe, so much so that the Wolves do not attempt to follow. The crippled Deer makes for some island sanctuary where he rests in peace till his leg is healed, or it may be, in some cases, till the freezing of the lake brings him again into the power of his foe.

Ungainly and very young, the caribou calf even at this age is able to run with the herd and outspeed the wolf.

These 6, then, were the cripples in hospital, and I hope our respectful behavior did not inspire them with a dangerously false notion of humanity. LIVES OF GAME ANIMALS, 1925–1927

Buffalo Hunt

I doffed the offending coat and we went forward as shown on the map. The horses were left; the wind was east. First we circled a little to eastward, tossing grass at intervals, but, finding plenty of new sign, went northerly and westward till most of the new sign was east of us. Sousi then led, telling me to step in his tracks and make no noise. I did so for long, but at length a stick cracked under my foot; he turned and looked reproachfully at me. Then a stick cracked under *his* foot; I gave him a poke in the ribs. When we got to the land between the lakes, Sousi pointed and said, "They are here." We sneaked with the utmost caution that way—it was impossible to follow any one trail—and in 200 yards Sousi sank to the ground gasping out, "La! la! maintenon faites son portrait au tant que vous voudrez." I crawled forward and saw, not one, *but half a dozen* Buffalo. "I must be nearer," I said, and, lying flat on my breast, crawled, toes and elbows, up to a bush within 75 yards, where I made shot No. 1, and saw here that there were 8 or 9 Buffalo, one an immense bull.

Sousi now cocked his rifle—I said emphatically: "Stop! you must not fire." "No?" he said in astonished tones that were full of story and comment. "What did we come for?" Now I saw that by backing out and crawling to another bunch of herbage I could get within 50 yards.

"It is not possible," he gasped.

"Watch me and see," I replied. Gathering all the near vines and twisting them around my neck, I covered my head with leaves and creeping plants, then proceeded to show that it *was* possible, while Sousi followed. I reached cover and found it was a bed of spring anemones on the far side of an old Buffalo wallow, and there in that wallow I lay for a moment revelling in the sight. All at once it came to me: Now, indeed, was fulfilled the long-deferred dream of my youth, *for in shelter of those flowers of my youth, I was gazing on a herd of wild Buffalo.*

 Then slowly I rose above the cover and took my second picture. But the watchful creatures, more shy than Moose here, saw the rising mass of herbage, or may have caught the wind, rose lightly and went off. I noticed now, for the first time, a little red calf; ten Buffalo in all I counted. Sousi, standing up, counted 13. At the edge of the woods they stopped and looked around, but gave no third shot for the camera.

I shook Sousi's hand with all my heart, and he, good old fellow, said: "Ah! it was for this I prayed last night; without doubt it was in answer to my prayer that the Good God has sent me this great happiness."

Then back at camp, 200 yards away, the old man's tongue was loosed, and he told me how the chiefs in conference, and every one at the Fort, had ridiculed him and his Englishmen —"who thought they could walk up to Buffalo and take their pictures." ARCTIC PRAIRIES, 1911

Travel

The Caribou is a travelsome beast, always in a hurry going against the wind. When the wind is west, all travel west; when it veers, they veer. Now the wind was northerly, and all were going north, not walking, not galloping—the Caribou rarely gallops, and then only for a moment or two; his fast gait is a steady trot, a 10-mile gait, making with stops about 6 miles an hour. But they are ever on the move; when you see a Caribou that does not move, you know at once it is not a Caribou, it's a rock.

We sat down on the hill at 3. In a few minutes a cow Caribou came trotting from the south, caught wind at 50 yards, and dashed away.

In 5 minutes another, in 20 minutes a young buck, in 20 minutes more a big buck, in 10 minutes a great herd of about 500 appeared in the south. They came along at full trot, lined to pass us on the southeast. At half a mile they struck our scent and all recoiled as though we were among them. They scattered in alarm, rushed south again, then, gathered in solid

The claws and positioning of feet of the great bears were important to an artist as technically minded as Seton.

body, came on as before, again to spring back and scatter as they caught the taint of man. After much and various running, scattering, and massing, they once more charged the fearsome odour and went right through it. Now they passed at 500 yards and gave the chance for a far camera shot.

The sound of their trampling was heard a long way off— half a mile—but at 300 yards I could not distinguish the clicking of the feet, whereas this clicking was very plainly to be heard from the band that passed within 50 yards of me in the morning.

They snort a good deal and grunt a little, and, notwithstanding their continual haste, I noticed that from time to time one or two would lie down, but at once jump up and rush on when they found they were being left behind. Many more single deer came that day, but no more large herds.

ARCTIC PRAIRIES, 1911

Moose Hunt

Scarcely two minutes had elapsed before I saw in a clearer space, some two hundred yards ahead, a great rusty red beast charging through the bush toward us. Into the snow I dropped like a shot. My companion saw nothing, but dropped because I did. On came the whirlwind of red hair, his body swaying in as he rounded the trees, like a racer turning a corner; head up, horns back, mane erect, a vision of tremendous brute strength as he dashed on toward us with that speed which is his greatest safety.

What thousands of thoughts of moose-killing rushed into my mind as I crouched on the snow, right on the trail, right in the path of the maned monster that was tearing through the timber toward us. It several times occurred to me that it was most likely he would kill me, but I lay still and bode my time. Then, just as he was within twenty yards of trampling on us, I **sprang to my feet**, shouting:

"Now, Jim!"

Bang-bang! went our rifles.

With a plunge the monster turned and started off again, crashing through the woods. My heart sank terribly as I

An almost destroyed painting of a bull moose, it still captures the ungainly nobility of this large, hoofed game animal.

thought how like this was to my former failures. But, strange to tell, the moose came to a dead halt only eighty yards away, in full view, and again stared at us. Then, in an imploring voice of terrible earnestness, I heard Jim behind me: "Oh, Seton! be careful this time!"

I took steady aim for his shoulder, and fired; then, as he again went off at his former furious pace, I sent a third ball whistling after him.

With feelings of mingled hope and fear we crossed over to his trail; and there—oh, savage glee! at every stride was a jet of blood. What a thrill of hope and triumph!

"Our moose, Jim, if I have to follow it to Brandon!"

"Not so far as that," said Jim, pointing to the crimson streaks.

And away we ran on the trail like wolves, fairly gloating over the continued jets of blood.

I had read so much of the tremendous distances that a moose will travel, even with a mortal wound, that I was prepared for a ten-mile run: but, to my surprise, before we had gone four hundred yards, Jim shouted: "Here he is!"

Sure enough, there he lay, with his knees doubled under him, like an ox in pasture. As we drew near, he looked back calmly over his shoulder.

"Guess we better bleed him," said Jim.

"Guess you better look out," said I. "I'd as soon go near a wounded lion."

"Well, let's give him a couple more balls."

So we both fired into him—without the slightest visible effect.

"Let's go round to his head."

Accordingly, we went around, keeping at a safe distance. Jim was about to fire when our victim's head drooped, then fell flat. I put a ball through his brain. His leg straightened out, he quivered, and lay still. The moose was dead.

Jim bled him. Then we stood for a few minutes, gazing on the magnificent beast, with feelings of rapture and triumph.

TRAIL OF AN ARTIST-NATURALIST, 1940

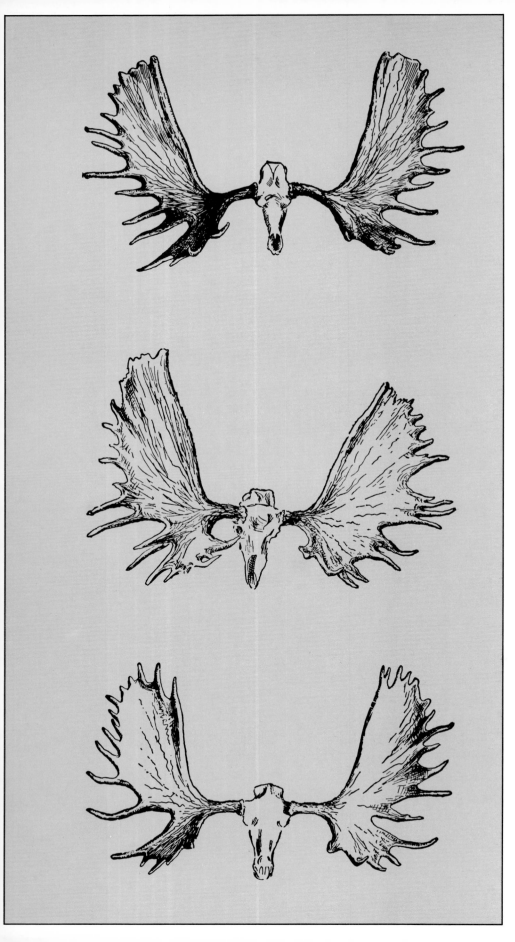

Moose

Ƀis summer life may have been spent on less than one hundred acres of swamp, but now he sets forth on his travels. Every few miles there is a sort of meeting-place of the sexes—a stretch of open woods—often a hardwood ridge between swamps. To these in turn he goes, nosing the earth and the wind for helpful suggestions. Standing with ears acock at every sound that might have been made by a Moose, and at length believing it to be from one of his own race, he challenges it with a deep, long grunt or a short bellow, and approaches it rapidly, slashing the brush with his horns to impress the other with the fact that he is a well-armed and fearless knight, circling about to try the wind from the stranger, or (if there be no wind) repeating his various calls and beatings of the brushwood.

There are two usual answers to all this— the long ringing reply of the responsive female or another deep grunt like his own, but varied with some guttural sounds that tell of a savage rival, who also is searching the woods with like object. In the latter case, there may be much grunting and maneuvering before they actually come together. As they approach they often express their defiance by slashing the brush with their new-grown spears and, when at last they meet and close with a crash, the spread and pointed antlers are at once their bucklers and their spears. It is rare to find a Moose horn without the dent of battle. I suppose that, without exception, every pair of full-grown Moose antlers has been in actual service "at the front," for every bull Moose hide has scars. In these combats the weaker generally saves himself by flight. It is but seldom that one of the knights is killed; yet this happens occasionally; and, as already noted, the battle has sometimes had a doubly fatal termination through the locking of the horns.

The record-bearer for spread among antlers of the Canadian Moose is the $68\frac{1}{4}$-inch pair taken by Dr. W. L. Munro, of Providence, R.I., on the Nepisiguit, N.B., October 12, 1907.

The previous record pair were those taken by F. H. Cook,

Old record heads. All three would still rank high as trophies.

of Leominster, Mass., in New Brunswick, October, 1898. These as measured by S. L. Crosby, of Bangor, at the time of capture, were 67 inches from tip to tip. During the intervening eight years they have shrunk a little, by inevitable drying, and today are only 65$\frac{1}{4}$ inches across. They now hang at Leominster, Mass., where I examined them.

Next comes a 66-inch pair, also from New Brunswick, now in the collection of Stephen Decatur, of Portsmouth, N.H., and after them a 65-inch pair from Manitoba, belonging to Otho Shaw.   LIVES OF GAME ANIMALS, 1925–1927

Musk Ox

On the 16th of August we left Lockhart's River, knowing now that the north arm of the lake was our way. We passed a narrow bay out of which there seemed to be a current, then, on the next high land, noted a large brown spot that moved rather quickly along. It was undoubtedly some animal with short legs, whether a Wolverine a mile away, or a Musk-ox two miles away, was doubtful. Now did that canoe put on its six-mile gait, and we soon knew for certain that the brown thing was a Musk-ox. We were not yet in their country, but here was one of them to meet us. Quickly we landed. Guns and cameras were loaded.

"Don't fire till I get some pictures—unless he charges," were the orders. And then we raced after the great creature grazing from us.

We had no idea whether he would run away or charge, but knew that our plan was to remain unseen as long as possible. So, hiding behind rocks when he looked around, and dashing forward when he grazed, we came unseen within two hundred yards, and had a good look at the huge woolly ox. He looked very much like an ordinary Buffalo, the same in color, size, and action. I never was more astray in my preconcept of any animal, for I had expected to see something like a large brown sheep.

My first film was fired. Then, for some unknown reason, that Musk-ox took it into his head to travel fast away from us, not even stopping to graze. He would soon have been over a

The heads of mature bulls show differences in antler configuration, especially as regards the brow tines.

rocky ridge. I nodded to Preble. His rifle rang; the bull wheeled sharp about with an angry snort and came toward us. His head was up, his eye blazing, and he looked like a South African Buffalo and a Prairie Bison combined, and seemed to get bigger at every moment. We were safely hidden behind rocks, some fifty yards from him now, when I got my second snap.

Realizing the occasion, and knowing my men, I said: "Now, Preble, I am going to walk up to that bull and get a close picture. He will certainly charge me, as I shall be nearest and in full view. There is only one combination that can save my life: that is you and that rifle."

Then with characteristic loquacity did Preble reply: "Go ahead."

I fixed my camera for twenty yards and quit the sheltering rock. The bull snorted, shook his head, took aim, and just before the precious moment was to arrive a heavy shot behind me rang out, the bull staggered and fell, shot through the heart, and *Weeso* cackled aloud in triumph.

How I cursed the meddling old fool. He had not understood. He saw, as he supposed, "the Okimow in peril of his life," and acted according to the dictates of his accursedly poor discretion. Never again shall he carry a rifle with me.

So the last scene came not, but we had the trophy of a Musk-ox that weighed nine hundred pounds in life and stood five feet high at the shoulders—a world's record size.

Now we must camp perforce to save the specimen. Measurements, photos, sketches, and weights were needed, then the skinning and preparing would be a heavy task for all. In the many portages afterwards the skull was part of my burden; its weight was actually forty pounds, its heaviness was far over a hundred.

ARCTIC PRAIRIES, 1911

The Musk

No one has yet located the source of the musk in this species; therefore, it is likely to be the produce of minute glands all over the skin. The practical elimination of the tail is very rare among bovines. In this

Seton sketched and painted the exotic musk ox on an incredible seven-month canoe trip into the Northwest Territories of Canada in 1907. The trip provided him material for his book Arctic Prairies.

family, the tail is usually specialized as a fly-flapper. In the Musk-ox it is, according to Richardson, reduced to 6 vertebrae, much as in the human species. Obviously, the Musk-ox has found a different and better solution of the fly problem.

It is worthy of remark that the Musk-ox has abandoned his tail and developed an intensely musky personality; the Musk-hog has abandoned his tail and developed a powerful musk-gland on his back; the Musk-deer has abandoned his tail and developed an overpowering musk-gland on his belly. All of these animals live in regions where mosquitoes are a pest; maybe the musk is developed for a protection against them.

The Yak furnishes further light on this, for he lives in climate and surroundings like those of the Musk-ox range. His home is cursed with mosquitoes, but, having evolved no musk, he has developed an enormous bushy tail for a fly-flapper.

The flesh of the Musk-ox is much like—like Buffalo indeed. When in prime condition, layers of fat are to be found on the neck, which is then the best part of the animal to eat. Sixty pounds did Hanbury get of this delicious flesh butter from one bull killed in August. But the fat does not form on the back as it does to make the back-fat in the Caribou.

There is, however, this one bad feature about the beef of this animal: It commonly bears a dominating, insupportable taint of musk. This is strongest in the old bulls, and least in the young calves; strong in the lean animals, and barely percepti-ble in the fat. But all are, in some degree, permeated with the musk at all seasons of the year.

On several occasions in August of 1907, I made a meal of Musk-ox beef. The musk was scarcely noticeable during the meal. But afterward, for hours, I had strong and unpleasant reminders of the experiment.

In 1907, I explored for 15 miles north of Aylmer Lake, and found only one Musk-ox and a few signs. In this region, 10 years before that (1898), Buffalo Jones had found them common.

The vast literature on the Musk-ox makes it possible to give details of its chosen home range. Primarily, it is an animal of the open, grassy, or scrubby plains of Canada, from the north edge of the woods to the sea. Its favorite food is grass; and favorite range the Northern prairies, on mainland or on Polar Islands, as far north as man has gone, that is, as far as there is land that is without an ice-cap in summer, and that, therefore, can grow grass.

Often, the whaler or explorer coasting along the rugged boulder-strewn hills, sees the dark brown form of Musk-oxen mixed with the huge round erratics of a bygone ice-day; and, when alarmed, the Musk-ox scampers up steep hills and over rocks at a rate that leaves men far behind. For they are surefooted as Goats, and far more active than common Cattle. Sometimes, the Musk-ox at the south edge of its range strays into the wooded belt. Oftentimes, it has been seen wandering for miles into the scattering spruce, and less often, its huge Buffalo-like form is seen plunging and browsing among the willow thickets that line some of our streams.

Hanbury found them in the scrubby spruce woods along Arkilinik or Thelon River, Aug. 12, 1901.

Roderick MacFarlane says that "during the severe cold of winter, the Musk-ox enters the outer sections of the forest, and is frequently found therein to a distance of 40 or 50 miles, while we have heard of more than one instance, where a stray animal had been killed at fully 100 miles from the nearest Barrens." These, like the pair recorded by Preble, from near Fort York, were mere stragglers.

Not often or far does it go, into dense swampy lands; and rugged mountains do not hold its affection for long; but it enjoys them for a season, and quits them only to drift to its proper home—the wide lush grassy plains, the prairies of the North.

As one ponders this account, the thought recurs: Does not every word of this apply to the Buffalo on its primeval range? Is not, indeed, the Musk-ox simply a Bison, a prairie Buffalo, environed in the North, and done into terms of polar surround-ings? LIVES OF GAME ANIMALS, 1925–1927

Fox

On May 15, 1882, as we drove over the prairie trail, my brother pointed to a yellow boulder some forty yards away on a hillside where were other boulders. "See," said he, "doesn't that look like a fox?"

I replied: "No; I see nothing but a yellow boulder."

But his eyesight was much better than mine, and he persisted: "That's a fox curled up."

With our noisy wagon and team, we marched past, within thirty yards; then when twenty yards beyond, a puff of wind seemed to make a crack in the boulder.

"That certainly is a fox," said my brother. He stopped, turned, and took one step from the trail toward the "boulder," which at once sprang up and ran for its life. A fox it was!

He skimmed across a stretch of burned black prairie; then, reaching a belt of unburned yellow grass 300 yards away, he crouched on this and watched us again; maybe because the grass was a good match for his own color, but more likely because it *was* cover.

I do not suppose he was asleep when first we saw him curled up among the boulders. He was probably watching us through his tail, trusting to his color; and would have lain still, hoping to escape detection, had not my brother alarmed him by leaving the trail and stepping in his direction.

Each time, the significant fact seemed to be that the fox *knew* he resembled the boulder or the grass, and was willing to take advantage of that resemblance.

TRAIL OF AN ARTIST-NATURALIST, 1940

Play

They played about, basking in the sun, or wrestling with each other till a slight sound made them skurry under ground. But their alarm was needless, for the cause of it was their mother; she stepped from the bushes bringing another hen—number seventeen as I remember. A low call from her and the little fellows came tumbling out. Then began a scene that I thought charming, but which my uncle would not have enjoyed at all.

Along with wolves and coyotes, the foxes were a favorite subject of Seton's. Here he depicts an unsuccessful stalk.

They rushed on the hen, and tussled and fought with it, and each other, while the mother, keeping a sharp eye for enemies, looked on with fond delight. The expression on her face was remarkable. It was first a grinning of delight, but her usual look of wildness and cunning was there, nor were cruelty and nervousness lacking, but over all was the unmistakable look of the mother's pride and love.

WILD ANIMALS I HAVE KNOWN, 1898

Prairie Red Fox

This animal is not much given to social amusements, but Norton and Stevens both tell me that on their fur farms in Maine it is a common thing for the Foxes to gather on moonlight nights and chase each other about with most uproarious barking and churring that do not seem to express anything but good-will and hilarity.

This species uses the smell-telephone much less, I think, than the Wolf does. Its principal method of intercommunication is doubtless by the voice. It has a short bark followed by a little squall like *"yap-yurr."* That is the sound oftenest uttered, but it has also a long yell and two or three different yowls or screeches as well as softer *churr-churrs* that doubtless have different meanings to its kind. The voice of the male is notably heavier and coarser than that of his mate.

There is a device that I have several times known the Ontario Fox to resort to when pressed by the hounds, that is, run along the railway ahead of a train, and cross a high trestle bridge. On one occasion I knew of a hound being thrown by the locomotive from the trestle into the river below, minus his tail, but otherwise unhurt. I was told, however, that all were not so fortunate, as some hounds had been killed at the same place in a similar way. It is very hard to say how much was intentional on the part of the Fox. The fox-hunters who know the animal, say *it was intentional throughout.* Some maintain that it was entirely accidental. It certainly was not necessary for the Fox to know anything about train times, as he could hear the train coming miles away. The track is a notoriously bad place for scent to lie, the trestle was a place of difficult footing, like a sloping tree, which often furnishes refuge, or the steep sand bank already noted, where I several times saw the Fox baffle the hounds. He might run to the train, just as I have known a Deer or Hare to run to a wagon or sleigh when flying for its life, preferring the unknown terror to the certain death. Add to this the element of luck when first the Fox made the attempt; success that time would lead him to try again.

No one can long watch a caged Fox in winter time without discerning the use to which it puts its great bushy tail. Its nose and pads are the only exposed parts, and those might easily be frost-bitten when it sleeps during severe weather. But it is always careful on lying down to draw these together, then curl the brush around them; it acts both as wrap and respirator. I have many times seen wild ones do this same thing, and am satisfied that the tail is a necessity of life to the Fox, as well as to the Squirrel and Wolf. I believe a Fox or Coyote would die before spring if turned out in the autumn without a tail.

LIFE HISTORIES OF NORTHERN ANIMALS, 1909

Red Fox

My experiences with the Springfield (Ont.) Fox (1888) gave me a large idea of the Fox's sporty mind. Night after night, when I went prowling with my hound, not to hunt but to learn things, one of the Foxes that lived nearby would give the Dog a run. At first it seemed like the ordinary chances of the hunt, but I soon found that the Fox would come to meet us if we were slow or late. Several times I sat down on a log to wait and listen, with the Dog at my feet, when from the near woods sounded the tantalizing "Yap, yap" of the Fox.

Away would go the Dog in full cry, but the weather was hot and the scent poor, and soon the Dog would come back panting to lie at my feet. Within three minutes the Fox would announce his return by his yapping bark, coming nearer and barking more loudly, till the tired Dog was led off on his fool's errand once more.

This game they played several times by daylight, and I had the pleasant experience of seeing how the Dog was fooled when the Fox wanted to get rid of him.

Reynard would lay his trail along a steep sandy cutbank that bordered the river. On dry sand, the scent is at all times poor, and in this case, the sand fell into his tracks so as apparently to destroy it altogether. At any rate, it was usually here that the Dog lost it.

On one occasion, I was hidden within 15 feet of that old dog-Fox, as he sat on his haunches to watch the Dog vainly looking for the trail on this bank, the Fox grinning to his ears as the Dog went searching about. He not only grinned, but,

Kit fox

Desert Fox

though quite unwinded, he uttered a loud panting noise that surely was a Fox laugh. In his eagerness to see the result of his trick-trailing, he several times stood up on his hind legs. I never had any question of a Fox's sense of humor after what I saw on those occasions.

All of this took place in June, July, and early August.

LIVES OF GAME ANIMALS, 1925–1927

Kit Fox

This diminutive Fox, no larger than a house cat, is a characteristic native of the Saskatchewan or upper Campestrian region. In Manitoba it was formerly found in the Pembina Hills and westward to the Souris. Alexander Henry, trading on the Red River in 1800–8, had one or two Kits brought to him from Pembina Hills, or, as he calls them, Hair Hills, nearly every season; one year, 1804–5, he had 57; of these, 26 were from Pembina Hills and 31 from Salt River. In 1873, Dr. E. Coues found Kit-foxes common along the Souris River at the Boundary Trail.

These are all the Manitoba records I can find, and since then the species seems to have disappeared from the Province, though it still abounds along the Saskatchewan and westward to the mountains.

It is strictly a prairie animal, harboring in burrows and never venturing far from them, so that it is the most subterranean of our Foxes.

Nothing is known of its mating, beyond the fact that the creature pairs, and that the pair continue together all summer, probably for life, as the male is active in the care of the young.

One of my guides, Lee Hampleman, of Meeker, Colo., tells me that in 1897, when on Pawnee Creek, Colo., he found a Swift's den. It was reached by a tunnel about 9 feet long and was 5 feet from the surface. The chamber was nicely lined with grass and contained 5 young ones. "Just the cutest, prettiest things he ever saw."

These were taken home to the ranch and easily raised, but they never became tame. Both parents were seen about the den.

LIFE HISTORIES OF NORTHERN ANIMALS, 1909

Some naturalists wonder if Seton or his publisher may not have miscaptioned the foxes. Seton's kit fox looks more like an arctic fox than a kit. The "desert" fox is now considered by taxonomists to be the common red.

But before we got to **Winnipeg,** I had a thrillsome experience. The poplar woods grew more thickly as we neared Pembina. Then we passed for miles through solid forests, with here and there an open space. As we neared St. Boniface, the eastern outskirts of Winnipeg, we dashed across a little glade thirty yards wide, and there in the middle was a group that stirred me to the very soul.

In plain view was a great rabble of dogs, large and small, black, white, and yellow, wriggling and heaving this way and that way in a rude ring. To one side was a little yellow dog stretched out and quiet in the snow; on the outer part of the ring was a huge black dog bounding about and barking, but keeping ever behind the moving mob. And in the midst, the center and cause of it all, was a great, grim, grisly wolf.

Wolf? He looked like a lion. There he stood, with his back protected by a low bush, all alone—resolute—calm—with bristling mane, and legs braced firmly, glancing this way and that, to be ready for an attack in any direction. There was a curl on his lips—it looked like scorn, but I suppose it was really the fighting snarl of tooth display. Led by a wolfish-looking dog that should have been ashamed, the pack dashed in, for the twentieth time no doubt. But the great gray form leaped here and there, and *chop, chop, chop,* went those fearful jaws, no other sound from the lonely warrior; but a death yelp from more than one of his foes, as those that were able again sprang back, and left him statuesque as before, untamed, unmaimed, and contemptuous of them all.

How I wished for the train to stick in a snowdrift now, as so often before, for all my heart went out to that great gray wolf; I longed to go and help him. But the snow-deep glade flashed by, the poplar trunks shut out the view, and we went on to our journey's end.

This was all that I saw, and it seemed little; but before many days had passed, I knew surely that I had been favored with a view, in broad daylight, of a rare and wonderful creature, none less than the Winnipeg Wolf.

The intricate pattern of hair on the hide of a wolf was a subject that fascinated the artist.

His was a strange history—a wolf that preferred the city to the country, that passed by the sheep to kill the dogs, and that always hunted alone.

In telling the story of *le Garou,* as he was called by some, although I speak of these things as locally familiar, it is very sure that to many citizens of the town they were quite unknown. The smug shopkeeper on the main street had scarcely heard of him until the day after the final scene at the slaughter-house, when he fell bullet-riddled on a pile of dogs that he had slain. That day his great carcass was carried to Hine's taxidermist shop and there mounted, to be exhibited later at the Chicago World's Fair, and to be destroyed, alas! in the Winnipeg fire that reduced the Mulvey Grammar School to ashes in 1896. TRAIL OF AN ARTIST-NATURALIST, 1940

Dog and Wolf

On November 25, 1882, about one o'clock, as I sat back after noonday dinner, gazing idly through the one unfrosted part of the pane, I was startled to see a large wolf dash toward our barns and into the cowshed, closely pursued by a black collie dog. I shouted: "Wolf!" then rushed out with my rifle.

The thermometer was far below zero, but I never once thought of that through all the chase which followed, although I went without hat, coat, or mittens.

By the time I got to the barns, the dog had driven the wolf out of the shed, and away they went over the snow. I fired a flying shot, but missed both dog and wolf; then joined in the chase which was the most scientific I ever saw made by a dog.

Every hundred yards or so, the dog overtook the wolf, and seized him behind. The wolf turned at bay. The dog then made a determined rush from the side next the woods. In other words, the dog took every care at each scuffle to prevent the wolf getting back to the wilderness, although the latter was straining all his powers to do so.

In this way, though the chase lasted for four miles, every fresh rush brought the wolf nearer to the settlement, until at last he stood within fifty yards of the house to which the dog belonged. The folks had seen them coming, and rushed out. The dog, now no longer fearing the fierce snaps of the wolf, and knowing he had all the help he needed, closed right in; and when I arrived, was holding him to the ground.

I stepped up close, and put a ball into the wolf's head; whereupon the dog, seeing his enemy finished, turned without a pause, dashed over the prairie as fresh as ever, and disappeared at full gallop; nor did he stop until, four miles away, he came to where he had left his master who was visiting at a friend's house. From this place it was he had driven the wolf home to kill.

This dog Frank was quite famous; his wind was obviously something unparalleled when he could run down a wolf, and still be quite fresh.

I was so struck by his prowess that I at once bought one of his progeny, which I kept for some time. It was pure Scotch collie.

For frontier life, collies are the best dogs in the world, taken all around; and I soon began to think—as every man does of his dog—that I had furthermore the best of all these best dogs.

I named him Bingo, after Franklin's dog in the old English nursery legend. Those who would know the rest of his life can find it in *Wild Animals I Have Known,* where I have told it with little embellishment, practically no deviation from the main historic facts. TRAIL OF AN ARTIST-NATURALIST, 1940

Gray Wolf

Although we must be cautious about receiving accounts of the Gray-wolf's ferocity, we are sure to be surprised by facts about its strength. I have known a young Gray-wolf, scarcely 6 months old, drag off a 100-pound bar of iron to which it was chained, taking it 200 or 300 yards without stopping and a quarter of a mile before discovered. This same cub could almost hold its own against an ordinary man pulling at its chain. I have several times seen a Gray-wolf in a trap go off with a drag that weighed considerably over 100 pounds . . .

TRAIL OF AN ARTIST-NATURALIST, 1940

Sketches of squirrels and martens from Lives of Game Animals are characteristic of Seton's astonishing ability to stop the subtle movement of sinuous, ever-moving creatures.

yellowstone Pk.

Br.

Br.

marten fossis.
from life by
Ernest Thompson Seton

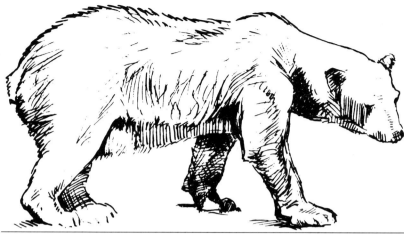

Wolverine

The Wolverine has shown his long trap-wisdom. Nevertheless, his doom is spoken. He has enrolled a host of enemies; for every hunter, trapper, and farmer on his range considers him a bandit, an atrocious robber, a creature of such malignity that he must be destroyed by any means, fair or foul, and at any time.

His magnificent robe is so much in demand now that the market-rating of choice pelts amounts to a bounty on his head.

The scarcity of game on his winter range during off-years for Rabbits often compels him to a step that amounts to suicide. As already pointed out, the famished Wolverine had no chance to learn discretion in the matter, and when he meets a Porcupine, he slays the dull Quill-pig, revels in its blood and meat. This stays his hunger—yes. But the arrows of death are in him, and a week or two later, the Quill-pig's revenge is complete.

He is nearly gone from the United States now. In southern Canada, he is become very scarce. In his own kingdom, the treeless North, he is found in fair numbers; but each year, the trappers and hunters swarm in every part of this range. It cannot be a question of many years before the wise and valiant Wolverine is known only by musty skins and dusty records.

The Wolverine is a tremendous character. No one can approach the subject of his life and habits, without feeling the same sort of embarrassment one would feel in writing of Cromwell or Tamerlane. Here, we know, is a personality of unmeasured force, courage, and achievement, but so enveloped in mists of legend, superstition, idolatry, fear, and hatred, that one scarcely knows how to begin or what to accept as fact.

Picture a Weasel—and most of us can do that, for we have met that little demon of destruction, that small atom of insensate courage, that symbol of slaughter, sleeplessness, and tireless, incredible activity—picture that scrap of demoniac fury, multiply that mite some fifty times, and you have the likeness of a Wolverine. LIVES OF GAME ANIMALS, 1925–1927

Canada Lynx

Although usually a shy creature, avoiding a meeting with man, the Lynx mother is very ready to fight for her family. On one occasion, while out on a camera hunt in Colorado, I heard a buck stamping in a little dale and, slipping off my horse, camera in hand, sneaked after the Deer. I found nothing but his tracks, and was peering across an open place, when I caught sight of a large animal close to me on the right. On passing into the clear space it turned to look at me. It was a Lynx, but it seemed very small, and its expression was one of innocent curiosity, entirely without menace. It paused at 30 feet. I hastened to adjust the camera, and as I did so a deep rumbling growl and a movement in a thicket close at hand made me jump. I turned around, to see within 15 feet a Lynx three times as big as the first, and eyeing me savagely from behind some willows. My first thought was to wish for a gun, for I realized that the Lynx in the open was only a kitten; now I had to meet the mother. My second thought was that the old one would do me no harm if I faced her, and did not molest the kitten. So I tried to get her photograph, but she disappeared, and when I looked around the little one also was gone. LIFE HISTORIES OF NORTHERN ANIMALS, 1909

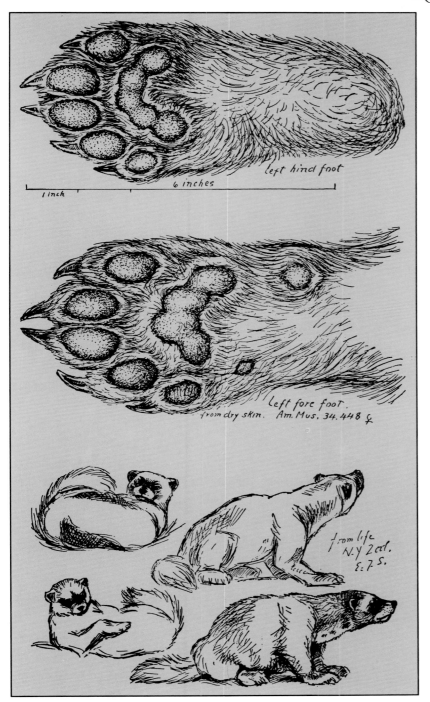

left hind foot

1 inch   6 inches

left fore foot.
from dry skin. Am. Mus. 34. 448 ♀

from life
N.Y Zo1.
E. 7. S.

Although the wolverine's tracks are unmistakably the tracks of a big member of the weasel family, they are so large that on a sandy beach one can mistake them at first for the tracks of the black bear.

Ferocity

Billy went "to market" yesterday, killing a nice, fat little Caribou. This morning on returning to bring in the rest of the meat we found that a Wolverine had been there and lugged the most of it away. The tracks show that it was an old one accompanied by one or maybe two young ones. We followed them some distance but lost all trace in a long range of rocks.

The Wolverine is one of the typical animals of the far North. It has an unenviable reputation for being the greatest plague that the hunter knows. Its habit of following to destroy all traps for the sake of the bait is the prime cause of man's hatred, and its cleverness in eluding his efforts at retaliation gives it still more importance.

It is, above all, the dreaded enemy of a cache, and as already seen, we took the extra precaution of putting our caches up trees that were protected by a necklace of fishhooks. Most Northern travellers have regaled us with tales of this animal's diabolical cleverness and wickedness. It is fair to say that the malice, at least, is not proven; and there is a good side to Wolverine character that should be emphasized; that is, its nearly ideal family life, coupled with the heroic bravery of the mother. I say "nearly" ideal, for so far as I can learn, the father does not assist in rearing the young. But all observers agree that the mother is absolutely fearless and devoted. More than one of the hunters have assured me that it is safer to molest a mother Bear than a mother Wolverine when accompanied by the cubs.

Bellalise, a half-breed of Chipewyan, told me that twice he had found dens, and been seriously endangered by the mother. The first was in mid-May, 1904, near Fond du Lac, north side of Lake Athabaska. He went out with an Indian to bring in a skiff left some miles off on the shore. He had no gun, and was surprised by coming on an old Wolverine in a slight hollow under the boughs of a green spruce. She rushed at him, showing all her teeth, her eyes shining blue, and uttering sounds like those of a Bear. The Indian boy hit her once with a stick, then swung himself out of danger up a tree.

Bellalise ran off after getting sight of the young ones; they were four in number, about the size of a Muskrat, and pure white. Their eyes were open. The nest was just such as a dog might make, only six inches deep and lined with a little dry grass. Scattered around were bones and fur, chiefly of Rabbits.

ARCTIC PRAIRIES, 1911

Use of Scent

The Wolverine undoubtedly follows the trapper because it is hungry and sees a chance of securing a bellyful. Having found food, it takes possession of it in a manner of wide usage. As already noted, small boys and Eskimaux take possession by spitting on the object, Squirrels by licking it, Foxes by urinating on it, and Badgers and several Weasels, including the Wolverine, by anointing it with the oil of their anal glands.

This is a potent method that carries strong conviction among most creatures that have retained unimpaired the sense of smell. If the Wolverine be not hungry, its provident instinct prompts it to put the possible food away for some day of worse luck, and, acting on the principle "better safe than sorry," it brands again in detail with its execrable odour the treasure trove; in so doing, other things, sticks, pots, etc., with an interesting odour of human grease, are accidentally touched with the oil, the convincing holy oil of the anal glands, and so, by a process not without parallel in other worlds, they are converted to its use and receive the honour of a cache into themselves.

It is not to be supposed that any part of the procedure is due to malice.

The inordinate sagacity of the species is, as with Wolves, largely fear born of sad experience, stimulated by any suggestion of human touch and assisted by nostrils of marvellous acuteness.

LIFE HISTORIES OF NORTHERN ANIMALS, 1909

Journal Entries

When in Toronto in 1881, preparing for this, my Western life, Doctor William Brodie, the naturalist, to whom I owe much, said to me: "Now, don't fail to keep a journal of your Western travels. You will be sorry if you omit this. And you will value it more each year." I began this at once. It is before me now. The first entry is dated: *Toronto, Ont., Monday, 13 Nov., 1881.* Saw three robins over the White Bridge.

I wonder if any one else ever got so much pure and subtle joy out of a simple statement as I did out of those first few words of record. They mean so little to others; but I felt instinctively that it was the beginning of what I wished to do. It was the first step into a glorious kingdom.

And I kept on doing it—still do so; and the Journal of my Travels and Doings is on my desk before me—fifty fat leather-clad volumes, most of them over-fat, and still increasing.

Scribbled in pencil, ink, water color, anything; smirched with the blood of victims sacrificed on the altar of the knowledge-hunger; burned with sparks of the campfire; greasy with handling by unwashed, hasty, eager hands; badly written; at times badly illustrated with hasty sketches—hasty, but meaningful. A bookseller would not give a dime for the lot, and I would not part with them for a double million. They represent more than anything else those sixty years of my life and thought, my strivings and my joy.

Aspiring young naturalists come to me for advice from time to time; and I always give them the counsel that helped me: Keep a full and accurate journal; and remember always Science is measurement.

But I now add to that some things that I did not then value at their true worth. "Collect specimens of all things that interest you, make drawings of those that are not easily collected, and label everything with at least the time and place.

"Write of each event on the day that it happened. Do not trust your memory. Let every page have place and date in full."

TRAIL OF AN ARTIST-NATURALIST, 1940

Lobo, the giant cattle-killing timber wolf Seton made world famous, was painted shortly after finally being trapped and killed by Seton in New Mexico, January 31, 1894.

"The Black Wolf" Currumpaw

by Ernest Thompson Seton

Rabbits and Lynxes

All wild animals fluctuate greatly in their population, none more so than the Snowshoe or white rabbit of the northwest. This is Rabbit history as far back as known: They are spread over some great area; conditions are favourable; some unknown influence endows the females with unusual fecundity; they bear not one, but two or three broods in a season, and these number not 2 or 3, but 8 or 10 each brood. The species increases far beyond the powers of predaceous birds or beasts to check, and the Rabbits after 7 or 8 years of this are multiplied into untold millions. On such occasions every little thicket has a Rabbit in it; they jump out at every 8 or 10 feet; they number not less than 100 to the acre on desirable ground, which means over 6,000 to the square mile, and a region as large as Alberta would contain not less than 100,000,000 fat white bunnies. At this time one man can readily kill 100 or 200 Rabbits in a day, and every bird and beast of prey is slaughtering Rabbits without restraint. Still they increase. Finally, they are so extraordinarily superabundant that they threaten their own food supply as well as poison all the ground. . . .

The Rabbits of the Mackenzie River Valley reached their flood height in the winter of 1903—4. That season, it seems, they actually reached billions.

Late the same winter the plague appeared, but did not take them at one final swoop. Next winter they were still numerous, but in 1907 there seemed not one Rabbit left alive in the country. All that summer we sought for them and inquired for them. We saw signs of millions in the season gone by; everywhere were acres of saplings barked at the snow-line; the floor of the woods, in all parts visited, was pebbled over with pellets; but *we saw not one Woodrabbit* and heard only a vague report of 3 that an Indian claimed he had seen in a remote part of the region late in the fall.

Then, since the Lynx is the logical apex of a pyramid of Rabbits, it naturally goes down when the Rabbits are removed.

This illustration, property of the New York Zoological Society, was done for a children's book on a cottontail rabbit.

These bobtailed cats are actually starving and ready to enter any kind of a trap or snare that carries a bait. The slaughter of Lynxes in its relation to the Rabbit supply is shown by the H. B. Company fur returns as follows:

In 1900, number of skins taken . . 4,473
In 1901, number of skins taken . . 5,781
In 1902, number of skins taken . . 9,117
In 1903, number of skins taken . . 19,267
In 1904, number of skins taken . . 36,116
In 1905, number of skins taken . . 58,850
In 1906, number of skins taken . . 61,388
In 1907, number of skins taken . . 36,201
In 1908, number of skins taken . . 9,664

Remembering, then, that the last of the Rabbits were wiped out in the winter of 1906—7, it will be understood that there were thousands of starving Lynxes roaming about the country. The number that we saw, and their conditions, all helped to emphasize the dire story of plague and famine. . . .

Let us remember that the Lynx is a huge cat weighing 25 to 35 or even 40 lbs., that it is an ordinary cat multiplied by some 4 or 5 diameters, and we shall have a good foundation for comprehension.

The uncatlike readiness of the Lynx to take to water is well known; that it is not wholly at home there is shown by the fact that if one awaits a Lynx at the landing he is making for, he will not turn aside in the least, but come right on to land, fight, and usually perish.

The ancient feud between cat and dog is not forgotten in the north, for the Lynx is the deadly foe of the Fox and habitually kills it when there is soft snow and scarcity of easier prey. Its broad feet are snowshoes enabling it to trot over the surface on Reynard's trail. The latter easily runs away at first, but sinking deeply at each bound, his great speed is done in 5 or 6 miles; the Lynx keeps on the same steady trot and finally claims its victim.   ARCTIC PRAIRIES, 1911

Wolf

A blood-red sun was sinking when I crossed Kennedy's plain, the snow was dyed crimson, a golden moon was rising through the eastern pink. The endless forest of poplars stood with their marble columns supporting a wide purple roof of thickly interlacing branches. It was so perfectly beautiful and so unmarred by the settler's axe that I wished I were not soon going back to Ontario.

The road lay for three miles through dense wood. When I was nearly through, I thought I heard my comrades shouting to me. I was surprised, as it was now night and late; I made the woods echo again with a shout, and then listened for the response. A long melancholy howl, and another, and another, and another.

"Wolves," I thought, and I mimicked their howling, and noted by the sound that they were gathering together, doubtless hunting. Then as they responded to my howls, I realized that they were rapidly coming nearer. "H'm," I thought, "it's me you are hunting, is it?" I was just leaving the woods; and as the sounds bore down nearer on my trail, I turned and stood perfectly still, thinking: "Well, if they mean to attack a man armed with a Winchester rifle, just let them come on." And so I waited.

Wolves had always been a favorite subject with me. Among the fine wolves at this zoo [Jardin des Plantes Ménagerie, in Paris] was one that frequently took a certain sleeping pose in one particular spot. This made sure of the model. So, on a two-foot by four-foot canvas, I made an oil painting of the obliging creature.

In one month of half days, the picture was finished, framed; and on March 20 delivered at the receiving door of the Grand Salon of Painting. There is always a great crowd at this, the final rush; and many artists are seen working on their canvases up to the last moment, when they turn them over to the receiving officers. Such crowds are always excitable but good-natured; and on this occasion, led by a famous and

"The Sleeping Wolf"—perhaps the greatest single animal oil painting ever done by Seton—was painted of a captive wolf in the Jardin des Plantes Ménagerie in Paris while the artist was a student at Julian's Academy.

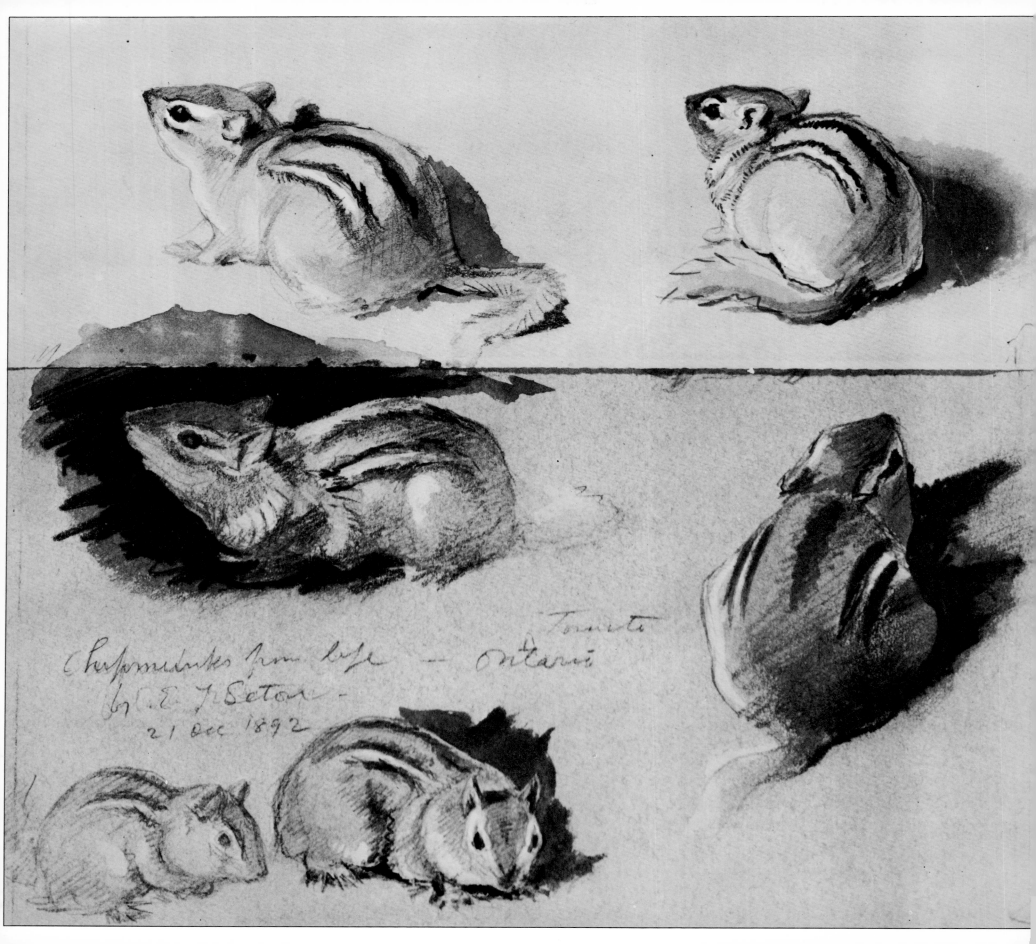

Chipmunks from life — Ontario
by E. T. Seton —
21 Dec 1892

Toronto

beautiful red-headed model named Sara Brun, they formed a procession and marched down the Champs-Elysées. But Sara's baton was a bright red parasol; and this, flourished in the air with wild whoops, looked a little too much like the red flag of anarchy. The police arrested Sara and broke up the procession.

There were about fifteen of us Americans that ran in the same bunch. Each, of course, was sending in a picture for the annual salon. We were all paired off for the dinner that was to follow; and for the "Vernissage," which is really the private view when the social world of Paris takes part.

It so happened that, on this occasion, Robert E. Henri and I were paired off; and when his picture was refused by the Hanging Jury, and mine, "The Sleeping Wolf," was not only hung but hung "on the line"—waist high, not skyed—it was an astounding event. At any rate, I had the delightful experience of taking Henri in as my guest at the banquet, and taking him in on my card at the Vernissage. He was, as he phrased it at the time, "simply my meat."

Those who know the history of American art will recall that, while I was still known merely as an illustrator, Henri rose to the topmost level of American painters. This seems to prove something, but I don't know what it is.

My picture, "The Sleeping Wolf," and my own interest in the animal, found a focus in a thrilling wolf story that was about this time in the daily papers.

TRAIL OF AN ARTIST-NATURALIST, 1940

Chipmunk

In Manitoba the common species appears above ground about the first or second week of April, that is, as soon as warm weather has surely set in. The regularity with which the Chipmunks appear, with the first soft wind of spring, sets me wondering sometimes whether there is not something more than mere verbiage in the phrase, "vernal influence." Snug in their deep, dark abode, far beyond reach of sun or frost, they cannot be reached or touched by mere temperature, nor can it be that they appear at a set time, as some of our winter-sleepers are said to do. No! They must come forth on the very day when first the very spring is in the land. A Chipmunk announces its return to sunlight in a manner worthy of a bird. Mounted on some log or root it reiterates a loud chirpy *"chuck-chuck-chuck."* Other Chipmunks run from their holes, for they awaken almost in a body, they run forth into the sunlight, and, seeking some perch, add their *"chuck-chuck-chuck"* to the spring salute.

This jubilant method of receiving the spring-time I have seen only in the eastern part of America, for the good reason that I never happened to be in the forest regions of Manitoba when the event should take place, but I am told by many that in our province the big Chipmunk fully maintains the tradition of its family.　　　　LIFE HISTORIES OF NORTHERN ANIMALS, 1909

Marten

This is the most arboreal of all our Weasels. It delights in climbing from crotch to crotch, leaping from tree to tree, or scampering up and down the long branches with endless power and vivacity. One cannot long watch a Marten, even in a cage, without getting an impression of absolutely tireless energy. For hours it will race up and down, leaping from perch to wall, to ground, to perch, to wall, to ground, to perch, over and over again, doing endless gymnastic feats, giving countless surprising proofs of strength, with bewildering quickness, all day long, without a sign of weariness, without a quickening of its breath. It must travel many hard miles each day in this way, yet it is complained that in confinement they suffer for lack of exercise.

Active as a Squirrel is an old adage, and yet the Squirrel is commonly the prey of the Marten.

It is remarkable that the Marten should follow the Red-squirrel in all its range, but hardly anywhere encroach on the territory of the large Gray- and Fox-squirrels—species which seem to afford special inducements to the active destroyer, for their numbers are great, it can follow into their holes, and their weight is so nearly that of its own that it would have no handicap in the leaps from tree to tree.

LIFE HISTORIES OF NORTHERN ANIMALS, 1909

All the perky, agitated movements of the chipmunk were captured in this series.

And the fall months passed, with the birds returning south and the plains animals gradually retreating southward until the first snows drove them away or underground . . .

Lynx studies
E. T. Seton
from photo.

Seton said in his autobiography that he painted this large oil trying to imagine how a pack of wolves would look from the rear of a speeding sleigh.

The northernmost cat, the lynx.

SETON
98

Dog

A thousand incidents might be adduced to show that in the north there is little possibility of winter travel without dogs and little possibility of life without winter travel. But April comes with melting snows and May with open rivers and brown earth everywhere; then, indeed, the reign of the dog is over. The long yellow-birch canoe is taken down from the shanty roof or from a sheltered scaffold, stitched, gummed, and launched; and the dogs are turned loose to fend for themselves. Gratitude for past services or future does not enter into the owner's thoughts to secure a fair allowance of food. All their training and instinct prompts them to hang about camp, where, kicked, stoned, beaten, and starved, they steal and hunt as best they may, until the sad season of summer is worn away and merry winter with its toil and good food is back once more. . . .

In some seasons the dogs catch Rabbits enough to keep them up. But this year the Rabbits were gone. They are very clever at robbing fish-nets at times, but these were far from the fort. Reduced to such desperate straits for food, what wonder that cannibalism should be common! Not only the dead, but the sick or disabled of their own kind are torn to pieces and devoured. Billy Loutit had shot a Pelican; the skin was carefully preserved and the body guarded for the dogs, thinking that this big thing, weighing 6 or 7 pounds, would furnish a feast for one or two. The dogs knew me, and rushed like a pack of Wolves at sight of coming food. The bigger ones fought back the smaller. I threw the prize, but, famished though they were, they turned away as a man might turn from a roasted human hand. One miserable creature, a mere skeleton, sneaked forward when the stronger ones were gone, pulled out the entrails at last, and devoured them as though he hated them.

I can offer no explanation. But the Hudson's Bay men tell me it is always so, and I am afraid the remembrance of the reception accorded my bounty that day hardened my heart somewhat in the days that followed. ARCTIC PRAIRIES, 1911

The artist wrote a number of dog stories and was as careful with their anatomy as he was with wild animals. During his art-school days in Paris he collected deceased dogs from the pound for dissection.

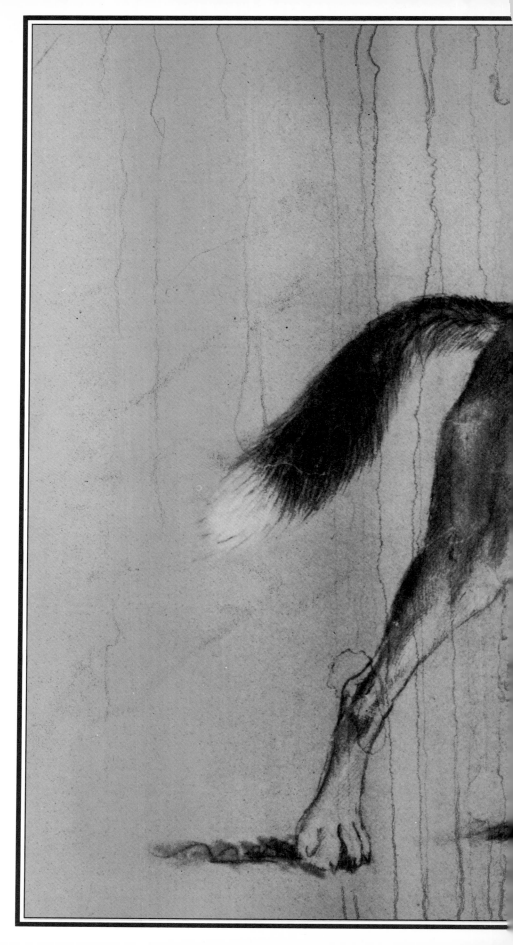

Fisher

The Fisher is a true Marten, endowed with all the tricks, activity, and the peculiarities of the race. It is probably our most active arboreal animal. The Squirrel is considered a marvel of agility, but the Marten can catch the Squirrel and the Fisher can catch the Marten, so that we have here a scale of high-class agility, with the Fisher as superlative. L. Warfield, after much experience, says this animal is capable of "jumping from tree to tree like a Squirrel, clearing a distance of 40 feet on a descending leap and never failing a secure grip." And there are several records of Fishers leaping to the ground from a height of 40 feet.

Again, on some illustrations, such as this ground squirrel, his technique was almost sterile and scientific—down to the proper leaves and fauna that made up the habitat.

In descending a tree it often comes down head first. But for the Monkeys and some others, we might believe it a rule that no creature is truly at home in the upper world till it *can come down head first* when it likes. Though so active in the tree tops, it is equally at home on the ground, and is so indefatigable and long-winded that it is known to run down Rabbits and Hares in open chase. If only it could swim and dive well, it would be the most wonderfully equipped animal in the world.

It has much of the blind pertinacity of the smaller Weasels. When I was at Rat Portage, in October, 1886, an Indian brought in a superb Fisher, fresh killed. He saw the animal chasing a Hare. The Hare, with the pursuer close behind, circled about him. He saw the Fisher several times, but could get no shot until the very moment when it sprang on the Hare; then he fired and killed both animals with the same charge.

Its courage, too, is of a high order. In my early days I more than once was told of Fishers—or Blackcats, as they were called in Ontario—which attacked boys and dogs that had disturbed them. I never saw one of these attacks, but they were generally believed in, for all the hunters and trappers entertain great respect for the prowess of this remarkable animal.

LIFE HISTORIES OF NORTHERN ANIMALS, 1909

Ground Squirrel

In a two-acre field of wheat at Carberry, Man., July 5, 1892, I counted 16 Ground-squirrels sitting up. I could not see those that were down on all-fours feeding, but it is safe to put them at double this number. There were at least 50 Ground-squirrels in that field, or 25 to the acre; and along the bank of Pollworth's slough, north of Carberry, in the early 80's, I have often seen as many as 50 Ground-squirrels within an acre, and there captured 20 in one hour with two traps. Even halving the lowest of these figures, we should have, at that time, a Ground-squirrel population of 20,000,000 on the prairies of Manitoba alone; which is a total area of 10,000 square miles. But the whole area of the Flickertails' range is 30 times this, so that 600,000,000 might be its total population in 1900.

That these estimates are not excessive is shown by the bounty records. At Carberry, in the year 1890, with bounties at 3 cents per tail, $1,180 was paid out. This represented 40,000 Ground-squirrels killed in the municipality of North Cypress (about 400 square miles), and yet there seemed to be just as many as before.

Carberry, Man., July 5, 1892. As the sun lowered, it fast lengthened the shadows, and brought into prominence the smallest depressions on the prairie; it revealed also on a long bank by the 20-acre wheatfield a perfect labyrinth of Ground-squirrel runs leading from all parts of the near prairie for 100 yards or more into the grain. The runs had no common plan beyond convergence at the crop; but each main run appeared to have on it a sort of refuge burrow at every 10 or 15 yards. These refuges differed from the residential burrows in being small, inconspicuous, half-hidden in the run, and without mounds. The Ground-squirrels would dodge from one to another, twinkling in and out of sight at the slightest alarm. If two happened into the same burrow, there was mischief brewed at once, and the weaker had to make a dash across country in search of some more hospitable retreat.

LIVES OF GAME ANIMALS, 1925–1927

Richardson's Ground Squirrel

This is by far the most abundant of the Ground-squirrels. At Whitewater on April 29, 1904, I examined an interesting colony of the species. In its centre of population I marked off a space 10 yards by 20, then counted the burrows in it. There were 50. This, I should think, meant at least 25 adult Ground-squirrels in the space of less than one twenty-fourth of an acre. The colony straggled along for a mile or more, the population thinning out on the level fields to four or five holes per acre, and of course with none at all in the wet places. But taking all together, I calculated the Ground-squirrel population at not less than 10 per acre, or, say, 5,000 to the square mile. That 10 per acre is not too high is shown in a case observed on the Saskatchewan by James M. Macoun. A farmer there killed 300 of these Ground-squirrels on his field of less than 10 acres, and yet it made no obvious difference in their numbers.

E. T. Judd tells of a square mile in North Dakota on which 4,000 Ground-squirrels were killed in one season.

LIFE HISTORIES OF NORTHERN ANIMALS, 1909

Striped Ground Squirrel

At Carberry, September 8, 1904, I dug out the Ground-squirrel nest from which I made the diagram. I did not see the rightful occupant, but suppose from its size and character that it was the work of a Striped-gopher. In one place, as marked, was found a salamander (*Ambystoma tigrinum*). It was not dormant but very sluggish. Several times have I found this species thus utilizing the burrows of the Ground-squirrels for its own winter den. These galleries were much plugged with soft earth and not easy to trace. Most were one and one-half to one and three-fourths inches wide, and about three inches down, but never more than six inches from the surface. I have also seen another burrow that is attributed to this species. It goes down nearly straight for a dozen feet. It may possibly be the winter den, but I never found the bottom or the animal that made it. The natives say it is a well, but I think they are mistaken.

In 1882, I published certain drawings of the prairie in section. They were the four faces of one square hole. The extent to which the burrowing rodents had recently interfered with the surface deposits was very plain, but later studies showed that most of these results were traceable to the Pocket-gopher (*Thomomys*). LIFE HISTORIES OF NORTHERN ANIMALS, 1909

Sea Otter

Of all the creatures living in the cold North seas, the Sea-otter is alone in that he usually swims on his back. Sailing, paddling, shooting or diving he goes, with his back to the deep, and his shining breast to the sky. But his neck is doublebent, so his big soft eyes sweep the blue world above and around. Propelled almost wholly by his big finlike hind feet, he moves with easy sinuous sweeps through the swell with its huge broad fronds of kelp—with back first, he ever goes forward, until the moment comes to dive—supple as an eel he turns—back up like a Seal or Beaver, and down he goes—down, down—long strings of silver bubbles mark the course, and by a strange atmospheric change, the color of the black merman now is yellow-brown as a seaman's slicker, or golden as a bunch of kelp. Down 30 to 100 feet or more he goes, and gropes around in the gloom, until he finds some big fat squid or sea-urchin. He does not hurry, for he can stay under 4 or 5 minutes. Then up he comes with the prey in his jaws, back to the top, to the borderland, that eternal line between the two kingdoms of air and water, on which he lives.

Here again on his back he lies, as, using his broad chest for dinner table, he tears open the sea beastie, feeds on its meat, and flings its shell aside, if it have any. Then he repeats the dive, and the feasting, until his sleek round belly is well filled. Now, among the heaving, friendly kelp he lazes on his back, plays ball perhaps with a lump of the leathery weed, tossing it from paw to paw, taking keen delight in his cleverness at keeping it aloft, as a juggler does his balls; and sniffing in disappointment if he should foozle the ball and miss the catch.

Other Sea-otters are about him, for Amikuk, like most fishermen, is of a neighborly spirit and loves good company. His mate may be there with her water baby in her big motherly lap. She tumbles it off into the deep for a swimming lesson; and round and under she swims to exercise "the kid," and make it learn. This is a very ancient game, this water-tag; the earliest monad that ever wriggled tail in the hot first seas, no doubt invented it. It is deep in everything that swims, or moves, and loves good company; so father Otter pitches in, and plays it, too. For half an hour they may keep it up. Father is still strong and frolicsome; so is mother; but the water baby is tired. Its big round eyes are blinking in weariness, and it is ready for sleep. Trust mother to look out for the little one. She curls up and takes it, not pick-a-back, but in the snug bed that she makes by curling belly up, as she floats among the weed. Her four feet are the bedposts, and in some degree the coverlet, too, for she holds it to her breast, crooning softly to it, till its whimpering ceases and it sleeps. Its fur may be wet and cold, but its skin is dry and warm; and drifting like a log of drift among that helpful wrack, they float, and love the lives they live.

But father is full of energy. He is one of thirty or forty that herd along this bed of kelp, that marks a deep-down feeding ridge, where their shiny seafood swarms. And away they go, in a race that recalls the tremendous speed and energy of the Porpoise in the sea. Undulating like water serpents, or breaking from the side of a billow, to leap in a long curve, splash into the high wet bank of the next. LIVES OF GAME ANIMALS, 1925–1927

The artist considered the sea otter—as have dozens of naturalists since his time—a fascinating and gentle creature.

Porcupine

May 1, 1882, I shot, at Big Moose Lake, a female Porcupine which contained a foetus that would certainly have been born within three or four days. It weighed 1¼ pounds avoirdupois (567 grm.), and measured in total length 11¼ inches (285 mm.), the head and body measuring about 7¾ inches (just 195 mm.). It was densely covered with long, black hair, and the quills on its back measured a little over half an inch (13 mm.) in length. The discoid placenta measured 2¼ inches (57 mm.) in diameter.

Concerning the further development of the young, I have no information beyond the fact that, early in August, I found young Porcupines half-grown in the Adirondacks, and already leading independent lives. What time they begin to leave the nest, whether they follow their mother and are cared for by her, and when fully grown, have not yet been recorded.

On the ground the Porcupine's best speed is slow, but it is fast compared with its movements in the branches. Here it goes about like a sloth, when it does move, often spending days in a single tree. In the water it floats because of its quills; each one is a little barrel of air to hold it up, and it manages to paddle in the desired direction to considerable distance. . . .

"The stupidest thing in the woods" is the descriptive verdict applied to the Porcupine by all who know it at home. It will waddle into almost any kind of danger, and eat almost any kind of food with utter oblivion of consequences.

At Ingolf, Ont., on September 16, 1904, in the woods near the railway I found a dynamite box and a stick of dynamite, one-third eaten by a Porcupine. There were no "Porky" remains near, so evidently he had not chewed hard enough.

You may drive the creature out of your camp with fire and sword, but that will not prevent its coming back, if able to crawl, within half an hour, to blunder into the same mischief as brought down vengeance before.

LIFE HISTORIES OF NORTHERN ANIMALS, 1909

EAST

Far more than miles separated the Manitoba prairies from the noise, filth, and crowded humanity that was New York City in 1883. And a young man of twenty-three—regardless of burning ambition and a considerable talent—was little prepared for life in that metropolis. Even art-school days in London—the great, gray, and civilized London—in no way prepared a man for the raw, unplanned, rapidly growing sprawl that was New York before the turn of the century. America, not much more than 100 years old, was growing like an annoying, ugly, and overfed brat— too healthy to slow down, too young and ambitious to know it was anything but beautiful, and far too unsophisticated to care.

But there was the excitement. No matter how a man of nature may hate living in the huge city and regardless of how many times he may leave for the solitude of his woods and fields, there is the excitement—drawing him back. And there is always the knowledge that one is where the important things are being done. New York, for the creative person, is what drugs are to the addict or alcohol to the drunkard. There is the surfeit, the disgust, the disillusionment, and a true hatred at times. Leaving is like throwing off an almost unbearable weight, and yet, in time, there comes the uneasy feeling that one is missing something—that one will grow out of touch. There is also the sensation that—after days of rest, quiet, and cleansing of the lungs and mind—it is *too* quiet. And when time begins to extend the length of days, when the bright edge of joy is no longer as acute as the sunrise or the sound of rain on leaves of oak and maple, it is time to return.

And at some point on the journey back—beginning ever so slowly—comes the feeling of a radiation of energy. The giant city—coarse, smoke-laden, foul-smelling and painful to the ears—is, nevertheless, a monstrous generator of human creativity. It is inconceivable that any one place on earth as small as the slender, rock-ribbed island—packed with millions of persons working, striving, thinking, *doing*—could be anything but a source of tremendous creative energy.

In the crowded, filthy streets near the business district, in cheap back rooms of soot-stained boarding-houses, and in the grimy shops where illustrators worked and printers toiled, there was fulfillment. After the years of frustration and lack of recognition there was acceptance. Pay was meager, but pay was never the end sought. There had always been the deep knowledge that the talent was deep enough—given a chance to unfold—if only there developed a need, a void to be filled.

There was the simple gratification in doing a sketch of a raven to be used as an illustration advertising a box of cigars . . . for the fortune of twenty dollars. Nights were spent in the quiet of a boardinghouse room writing animal stories—about foxes, snowshoe rabbits, and drumming grouse—which were as much a part of the man as breathing. Illustrating came as naturally as walking. One had but to close the eyes and back came the plains of Carberry and the marshes of the Don River— with the beloved birds and animals, so deeply missed and yet there in color and shape as though a few yards away.

St. Nicholas Magazine accepted his stories, and the joy of seeing the sketch of the meadowlark and the brief description of the encounter in 1882 on a Manitoba prairie was so exquisite as to be almost painful. It was a beginning, a breathless glimpse into what might be a world where everyone knew what was deeply known inside, that there was so much to give, and so much of it good. Nights at the Art Students League were filled with the turmoil of laughter, sketching, and the friendship of other young aspiring artists—many of whom would go on to fulfillment in their own fields. Sundays saw long walks in Central Park or through the quiet streets, sometimes just getting out for exercise after being cooped up for hours over a drawing board or writing pad. There were evenings with friends from Toronto and from art-school days in London and occasionally a cheap ticket to the theater—Edwin Booth as Shylock, Emmet in *Fritz* and Lily Langtry in *Peril.*

But frequently came the sudden constriction of the spirit and the need to flee the grime, noise, and press of humanity. Back to Carberry for the spring—for it is in the spring that New York most becomes a prison for those raised in the open spaces. And the sandflowers were back on the sandhills and waterfowl darkened the skies and the spirit expanded again—for a short while. The long summer ends and September sees the goldenrod begin to turn brown with the first frosts. A few days in Toronto with family and it is back to the city—which, strangely, does not seem as much a prison now that autumn days bathe the tall spires and the smell of burning leaves floats across Central Park. Fall brings a feeling of urgency and a heightened sense of awareness.

There are illustrations—pen-and-ink and pencil drawings—by the scores that will be used in children's books—*Bird World,* by J. H. Stickney, printed by The Athenaeum Press; *Bird Portraits,* by Ralph Hoffman, printed by Ginn and Company. The plates of beloved birds—the song sparrow, flicker, kingbird, wood thrush, goldfinch, golden-crowned kinglet, and the chickadee—were reproductions whose clarity reflected a sureness of anatomical detail gained from years of dissection and authentic habitat background notes from precious diaries.

And with each page of illustration—animals for *Four-Footed Animals,* by Mabel Osgood Wright, edited by Frank Chapman and published by the prestigious Macmillan Company—came the calm knowledge that the preparation had been right . . . and the years of study and practice were enough to make it better—so much better later. Plates of mule deer, the varying hare, the front paw and tail of a muskrat, the buffalo, a red fox hunting—all poured from the drawing pad to the engraver as water from a deep, pure, and powerful spring . . . coming from a deeper underground source as yet not fully tapped.

With the satisfaction of work done well came the friendships—with Dr. J. A. Allen, Curator of Birds, American Museum of Natural History, and his assistant, Frank M. Chapman; with C. Hart Merriam, and Henry M. Steele of Scribner's; and with W. Lewis Fraser, of *The Century Magazine,* who ordered a thousand drawings for the publication.

A need for more knowledge brings a voyage to Paris and more art training at Julian's Academy on the Faubourg St. Denis—mornings filled with sketching and afternoons painting animals at the Jardin des Plantes Ménagerie. Nights in a top-floor apartment at the small residential Hôtel de l'Univers, finishing a painting of a sleeping wolf—and another of wolves gnawing on a skull. The days of art students' noise blend with the painstaking detail of animal anatomy—dissection of dogs, cats, horses, cattle . . . and the eyestrain of painting and sketching in poor light. The wolf paintings hang in art galleries in Paris and Toronto—amid mixed reaction—and one goes on to hang at the Chicago World's Fair in 1893.

Life is work and life is travel—travel from Paris to London and New York, and New York to Carberry and Toronto, but always back to New York, where others' books wait for illustrations and the writing of one's own books awaits—always behind schedule in a world moving with such speed. *Studies in the Art Anatomy of Animals* is published and the years of detailed anatomical study fall behind. The years of fascination with wolves bear fruit with a chance to travel to the Southwest. There, in the rolling, piñon-dotted foothills of northeastern New Mexico, are the wolves one has dreamt of for a lifetime. There are the cowboys, the frontier towns, the cattle, and the raw, beautiful land that suddenly feels as though it has been waiting for this day. . . . Days of incredibly blue skies and hard, glaring sunlight on saddles, guns, traps, and wagon fittings blend into evenings of sunsets with colors only before imagined. And the coyotes' night songs were now interspersed with the full-throated howls of the great prairie wolves, wreaking vicious havoc on the range-free cattle.

Days of trapping and tracking are new experiences, and the dry, dusty land brings out an awareness of space. After the stifling city, the blue-domed land renews vigor in daily living and days in the saddle bring back a lust for life which had been growing dormant in the East. From the baits and poisons and the cowboys comes the basis for Lobo and Blanca—hero and heroine of later books and short stories. And a return to the city looms all too close.

Upon the return and a voyage to France on the S.S. *Spaarndam,* the meeting with the woman, Grace, and her mother—the beginning of a long voyage which was to reshape lives. Marriage two years later to Grace was the introduction to a world long ignored—a world of elegance, travel, companionship, and then a child. Throughout all, there was the city and the writing and the art—as each year saw more books in print and a growing sense of participation in the affairs of the day. Familiar friends slowly began to take on names known in circles of art and writing, and in the world of science.

Time finds a man when it is ready, and fame and success fall upon one when he is prepared to assume them.

Houses in New Jersey, apartments in New York, and homes in Connecticut slide as pieces into the jigsaw puzzle of a life. A dislike for city living remains, but formal affairs could be faced with far more ease than in years earlier and, though a disdain for apparel is still present, a wardrobe was accepted with ever greater tolerance and casual elegance became more a natural manner of life.

There was the intense love for the girl child and the joy of watching her grow among the wildlife near the big stone house close to the lake. Baby skunks and pet chipmunks are as much a source of wonder to her as they were to the boy in Lindsay forty years before. Nature is a rediscovery for a parent, and the world of the spotted salamander, the tiny red newt, the leopard frog, the painted turtle, and the bluejay becomes a reawakening. Stories told to one child make easy telling to others and words for children's books are not difficult to find. The companionship of a woman well schooled and well bred, yet willing enough to ride, camp out, and shoot like a man, could be stimulating. The companionship of the same woman, strong-willed, independent, and at times competitive, could be equally as stimulating—and irritating to a man long used to his own way.

The success years tumble over one another as the child grows and work becomes a possessive thing. Scientific volumes seem always on a deadline—yet finally appear in print. *Lives of Game Animals* wins great recognition and awards follow awards: Naturalist to the Government of Manitoba; The Smithsonian; the Biological Survey; The American Museum of Natural History's claim of best animal and bird painter of the day; Member of the National Institute of Arts and Letters; The Elliott Gold Medal of the National Institute of Sciences; The John Burroughs Gold Medal; and the Gold Medal of the Camp Fire Club of America.

Formal dinners in New York are shared with the great and near-great, and correspondence and visits with

Theodore Roosevelt, William Hornaday, John Burroughs, and Frank Chapman are frequent occurrences.

And yet . . . there remains the void . . . the uneasy feeling, in spite of fame, economic security, myriads of old friends, and days in comfortable surroundings, that something is left undone—in another time and another place.

For the mother of the child, the companion of thirty years ago, has grown away from him, with her world travels and communication a forgotten thing. With creeping time comes the realization of age . . . for which one is never ready. With so much yet undone there also comes annoyance at the demands upon time and the clutter men make of their lives in the name of obligation, responsibility, and ambition.

There comes the time when the years past all merge into an unbroken curve below—as though forming the slope climbed on the way to the peak . . . almost, but not quite, within sight. And at that same time perhaps there is the question . . . is the peak worth striving for—has it been worth it from the beginning . . . was this the right route? Is there another and perhaps better way?

The greed and dishonesty of people suddenly seem more obvious. The damp cold of eastern winters penetrates to the marrow as it did not the previous year, and the huge city—for the first time since entered by a confident young man from the Canadian prairies forty-seven years ago—seems again filthy, noisy, cold, cruel, and inhospitable.

To mind come the blue-domed skies and the white glare of the sun bathing a dry, baked landscape where the air is clear, wild things beckon and, perhaps, youth can be regained, if only for a few years.

For the buffalo wind—the siren call answered so many times before—is blowing again. And this time there is a new insistence in its call—and one best not ignored. . . .

JOHN G. SAMSON

Commonly called a clay-colored sparrow today, this one was sketched by Seton for a book by Frank Chapman.

Whitetail Deer, Bluejay, Chickadee, Fox,
Northern Flying Squirrel, Red Squirrel, Cottontail, Rabbit, Mink,
Beaver, Woodchuck, Raccoon, Muskrat, Opossum

Whitetail Deer

It is essentially a creature of the denser woods and thickets where these alternate with open glades. Bare plains and rugged hillsides are an abomination unto it; but every Western river whose long flood-flat is belted and patched with far-reaching scrubby thicket is sure to carry with it a long-drawn-out population of skulking Whitetails, which, between scrub and bog, are able to hold their own and multiply, in spite of rifle and Wolf; while the hill-frequenting Blacktail is rapidly passing away.

In the hard-wood ranges of the East, this preference is less observable because all of the country is one thicket, but the life of the animal is the same, and its chosen resort is the border-land between sunny open and friendly cover.

In one other way the Whitetail is peculiar: It prefers the edges of civilization. There man wars on its foes, the Wolves; his axe makes sunny openings in the fir gloom; and, above all, his crops furnish delectable food in time of scarcity. In all parts of the North and East, therefore, the Whitetail has followed the settler into the woods and greatly extended its range thereby. In this we see the reasons of its extension into Manitoba and northern Ontario.

Some of the most remarkable variations are here shown. The record for points still rests with a pair owned by Albert Friedrich, of San Antonio, Texas, which are of such super-abundant vigor as to have 78 points. The 42-pointer from the Adirondacks and the 35-pointer from Minnesota claim second and third places, respectively.

Antlers are sexual appendages, and their connection with the genital system is close, though obscure. The latter cannot be deranged without creating a disturbance in antler production, and the effect of emasculation is extraordinary. Judge Caton, to whom we are so much indebted for light on the Deer family, shows that a buck castrated when his antlers are nearly grown will drop them within thirty days after. Next year he will grow a new pair, according to rule, but they never ripen,

harden, or peel. They continue full of blood and life until they are frozen and broken off by accident, leaving a stump. Each year thereafter the stump will grow larger and a new antler is projected, but never finished; and each succeeding year the antler will be smaller and more irregular.

Wolves, too, rank high in the list of the Whitetail's foes, and have long played seesaw havoc with the Deer in the North. On the Upper Ottawa the Deer came in with the settlers. The Wolves followed, because in the Deer they found their winter support. In summer the Deer were safe among the countless lakes, and the Wolves subsisted on what small stuff they could pick up in the woods. But winter robbed the Deer of the water safe-havens, and then the Wolves could run them down; thus they wintered well.

But wintering well meant increasing, and the Wolves became so numerous that they destroyed their own support, when starvation, followed by extinction, was their lot. Again the Deer recovered locally or drifted in from other regions, and again the Wolves increased to repeat their own destruction. This has been the history of the Deer population along most of our frontier wherever winter is accompanied by deep snow. If we could exterminate the Gray-wolf we should half solve the question of deer-supply; but there is no evidence that we shall ever succeed in doing this.

In mid-December, after this annual climax of their lives is over, the jealousies, the animosities, the aspirations of the males, the timidities and anxieties of the females are gradually forgotten. The Mad Moon wanes, a saner good-fellowship persists, and now the Whitetails—male, female, and young—roam in bands that are larger than at any other time of the year. Food is plentiful, and they fatten quickly, storing up (even as do Squirrel and Beaver) for the starvation-time ahead—only the Deer store it up in their persons, where it is available as soon as needed, where it helps to cover them from the cold, and whence it cannot be stolen, except "over their dead bodies," by a burglar stronger than the householder himself.

They wander thus, in their own little corner of the wilderness, till deepening snows cut down their daily roaming to a smaller reach, and still deeper till their countless tracks and trails, crossing and recrossing, make many safe foot-ways where the food is best, though roundabout them, twenty feet away, is the untrodden and deep-lying snow, that walls them in and holds them prisoners fast until its melting sets them free to live these many chapters over again.

There is no probability that the Whitetail will ever serve man in any domestic capacity, but it will always have a value by reason of its singular adaptability and gifts. It is the only one of our Deer that can live contentedly and unsuspectedly in a hundred acres of thicket. It is the only one that can sit unconcernedly all day long while factory whistles and bells are sounding around it, and yet distinguish at once the sinister twig-snap that tells of some prowling foe, as far away, perhaps, as the other noises. It is the only one that, hearing a hostile footfall, will sneak around to wind the cause, study its trail, and then glide, cat-like, through the brush to a further haven, without even trying to see the foe who thus gets no chance for a shot. It is the least migratory, the least polygamous, the least roving, as well as the swiftest, keenest, shyest, wisest, most prolific, and most successful of our Deer. It is the only one that has added to its range; that, in the North and West, has actually accompanied the settler into the woods; that has followed afar into newly opened parts of New England and Canada; that has fitted its map to man's, and that can hold its own on the frontier. LIFE HISTORIES OF NORTHERN ANIMALS, 1909

Bluejay

One day I found a bluejay's nest. It was up high in the forks of a sapling, and was a very flimsy structure. The young in it were well grown and nearly fledged. Very discreetly, the old birds did not show up at first; but as soon as I began to climb the tree, they came sailing

A herd of deer bound away from the edge of a beaver-dam meadow — indicated by the beaver-cut aspen stumps. The deer are unidentified, but the scene is eastern.

Robin

about and swooping over my head, uttering in their loudest tones an *exact imitation* of the redtailed henhawk's scream. It was so close and so unlike the ordinary bluejay note that it flashed on me that they were trying to frighten me away with the note of a bird of which they themselves were dreadfully afraid.

This was one of the best attempts at deceit I ever met with in bird life; and like all other bluejay manifestations, shows the species to be a bird of unusual mental gifts.

TRAIL OF AN ARTIST-NATURALIST, 1940

Chickadee

They had still the assurance that winter would·end. So filled were they with this idea that even at its commencement, when a fresh blizzard came on, they would gleefully remark to one another that it was a "sign of spring," and one or another of the band would lift his voice in the sweet little chant that we all know so well:

another would take it up and re-echo:

and they would answer and repeat the song until the dreary woods rang again with the good news, and people learned to love the brave little Bird that sets his face so cheerfully to meet so hard a case.

But to this day, when the chill wind blows through the deserted woods, the Chickadees seem to lose their wits for a few days, and dart into all sorts of odd and dangerous places. They may then be found in great cities, or open prairies, cellars, chimneys, and hollow logs; and the next time you find one of the wanderers in any such place, be sure to remember that Tomtit goes crazy once a year, and probably went into his strange retreat in search of the Gulf of Mexico.

LIVES OF THE HUNTED, 1901

Only the surest of sketch artists could have captured, accurately, the unusual positions of robins—such as the preening pose in the lower right.

Fox

If we mix equal parts of Red-fox, Coon, and Bobcat, and season the combination with a strong dash of Cottontail Rabbit, we shall have the Gray-fox's disposition synthetically produced. He is shy, he is cunning, he is a desperate fighter when at bay, he loves the trees, and yet rejoices in the briar bush, he can run for hours and is an adept at trick-tailing, but will hide in a burrow or up a tree; and the places he frequents are the places where any one of these animals also may be found.

As I read the classic pages of Audubon and Bachman, I note that they say the Gray-fox is "shy and cowardly." Reference to a long list of natural histories reveals the fact that every animal treated in this book is by someone described as "shy and cowardly." The truth is, I take it, that no animal is such. All animals are brave, for I do not know of one—with the possible exception of the Opossum—that will not fight to the death when brought to bay, no matter how numerous or powerful his foes may be. What is there of cowardice in a helpless Gray-fox of 10 pounds weight running away from 20 large hounds each 60 pounds, backed by half-a-dozen hunters each 150 pounds of weight, on half-a-dozen horses each 1,500 pounds weight, and armed too often with guns and pistols into the bargain?

Discretion is the better part of valour; the valiant Gray-fox is discreet. But do you want to see a fair fight and make a just appraisal of courage? Select a 10-pound Dog and match him against a 10-pound Fox. Then you will have no cause to charge the Fox with cowardice. Indeed you will have to play special Providence if you would save your Dog from destruction. Yes, go a step farther. You—a 150-pound man, we will suppose—go into the arena alone and armed only with nature's weapons, and grapple with a 10-pound Gray-fox— if you dare; and see which of you will come out free of the taint of cowardice.   LIVES OF GAME ANIMALS, 1925–1927

The inquisitive red fox was always one of the artist's favorite subjects. They were around him in Canada during his youth, close to him in the East when he lived in Connecticut, and always present in the West.

Northern Flying Squirrel

I have no direct evidence on the home-range of this species, but analogy with other Squirrels and the absence of any migratory habit lead me to believe that the Flying-squirrel is content with a domain of approximately two or three acres.

In my Connecticut home woods I have more than once found three Flying-squirrel (*volans*) nests within a radius of fifty yards. This instance sheds some light on the creature's abundance—three families within two acres; and therefore I should say that here the Flying-squirrel is more abundant than the Red-squirrel, and yet is rarely seen. Its secretive nocturnal habits lead many to believe that it is not found in their locality, even though it may be the most numerous of its group.

I never knew of more than one family together in the nesting time, but in December, 1882, I found 9 adults living in one stub at Carberry. They were so close together that a rifle ball fired by my companion at the stub below their hole killed 4 and wounded another of the 9. They undoubtedly were profiting by each other's company for warmth, therefore this animal is somewhat sociable. The kindred species is well known to nest in colonies where some specially favorable spot is discovered.

The cry of this species is said to be like that of *volans,* which is a prolonged squeak not unlike the complaint of a red-eyed vireo whose nest is threatened.

My observations on *volans* tend to show that that species pairs, and that the male takes an active interest in the young. I have not been able to watch *sabrinus* at the season of reproduction, but analogy prepares one to believe that in domestic matters it is as good as its near relative.

The usual nesting place is a deserted hole, but any hollow tree will serve.

The young number from 3 to 6 and are born about the last of April.
LIFE HISTORIES OF NORTHERN ANIMALS, 1909

Red Squirrel

The home range of each individual is, I should say, less than ten acres. At Duff's Lake, near Carberry, is a grove of oaks that cannot cover much more than twenty acres, and it is yet range enough for a number of Red-squirrels to live in year after year. This grove is quite isolated; the Squirrels, to get to it originally, may have had to cross half-a-mile of bare prairie.

But the Red-squirrel knows so well how to use a hole in the ground that it can make these open journeys safely, when a more strictly arboreal animal would surely come to grief.

In a grove of thirty or forty oak trees, east of Carberry, Willie Brodie and I, on November 26, 1882, ran down and captured a Red-squirrel, that might easily have escaped to thicker woods farther away, but this small grove was evidently the home region that it knew, and here it would stay. In Ontario I have known one of the species to take up its abode in a barnyard, and never leave this all winter to go even fifty rods away.

Many a one passes its whole life in an orchard of from four to five acres. A family of Red-squirrels that I watched for some months at Tappan, New York, never, so far as I could learn, went a quarter of a mile from the central home trees.

In the woods about my Connecticut home is the Red-squirrel family elsewhere referred to as the "Singers." These I watch each summer, but I have never seen them one hundred yards from the home tree. If they ventured so far they would be trespassing on the occupant rights of the next Squirrel family, and be forced to fight or run away. I have, however, observed another family in northern New York that habitually travel along the fence between a corn-crib and a woods over a quarter of a mile off.
LIFE HISTORIES OF NORTHERN ANIMALS, 1909

Whether red squirrels or flying squirrels, the artist has again with camera-shutter sketches caught them in the peculiar, nervous, and never-at-ease poses which are so typical.

Merlin, by
Ernest Thompson Seton
31. nov. 1891

The debris and grime of Manhattan, the sooty squabbling English sparrows and soiled pigeons, faded away into the rough lichen-covered stone walls of Connecticut farmland, where, amid the incredible changing leaves of fall, the perky bluejay flitted and the gray and red squirrels bustled...

The merlin, whose circumboreal counterpart in North America is known as the pigeon hawk, appears a number of times in Seton's sketchbooks.

merlin . Paris .

Snowshoe from life

Ernest Thom

Cottontail

This is essentially a species of the borderlands, neither forest nor plain. It is fond of places overgrown with young pines, thickly crowded together, or thickets of briers and brambles. It rejoices in ill-kempt farms and plantations; and occupies, by preference, the coppices and grassy spots in the neighborhood of cultivation. But it is not contented with a home in unbroken forest.

All who have watched individual Cottontails closely, are struck by the smallness of their home range. I think it is probable that a Cottontail, unless driven afar by hounds or Foxes, spends its whole life within the limits of an acre.

It usually has a routine that it holds to for days at a time, following the same little paths, and feeding at the same places; so that, if you saw a Cottontail at a given place last night, you are likely to see it there again this evening.

Like all Rabbits, the species has regular pathways which it follows. These it incidentally improves by wear, as well as by cutting such new growths as tend to block them.

The Cottontail is the big game of the small boy. Be he trapper, chaser, or gunner, the first great triumph in his caveman life is usually the taking of a fat Bunny.

Found in nearly all parts of the United States, able to maintain itself on and about the farm—even on the prairies—this is the one game creature worthy of the name, that we have always and everywhere with us.

In the Northeastern States, the Cottontail is pursued with Dogs, and either shot on the run, or taken by hand from the stone wall, hollow tree, or Woodchuck hole to which it may have been driven.

In the Southern States, the creature is generally hunted with pointer Dogs, then routed from its form under the brushpile or the brier patch, and shot as it bounds away.

Bunny is wholly guileless in the matter of a trap. A snare placed on the trail, or in the gaps of some fence, is, soon or late, the Rabbit's undoing. A box-trap with apple bait set in the barnyard or in the near woods, is another plan that every small boy uses.

Greenwich, Conn., June 18, 1914. At 7:40, as I went through the woods at dusk, a Cottontail hopped on to the path. He froze; so did I. I glanced at my watch, and timed him. For 2 minutes 35 seconds, he never budged nor winked, so far as I could see.

Then he sank down on his hindquarters, and continued unmoving until 5 minutes was up. Now he seemed to shake a mosquito from one ear, but continued until 8 minutes 30 seconds had passed, when he again shook one ear. After a few seconds, he repeated the shake, and at 7:55 he hopped away. During all this time (15 minutes), I had stood, and moved but little, except to kill some mosquitoes.

Another note, made Jan. 18, 1905, implies that the Cottontail never winks, or else does it too quickly for observation. "To-day, I watched a near-by Cottontail for $2^1/_2$ minutes, and it did not once wink. I have never seen a Cottontail wink, or close its eyes. When I struck a sharp blow on a near board, the creature seemed to droop the upper lid a fraction of an inch, but not more than one-tenth of the distance necessary to cover the eyeball."

Again: *June 13, 1906.* To-day, I watched a Cottontail that froze $6^1/_4$ minutes. Then I got tired. He did not even wink, so far as I could tell. LIVES OF GAME ANIMALS, 1925–1927

Rabbit

The low rasping went past close at hand, then to the right, then back, and seemed going away. Rag felt he knew what he was about; he wasn't a baby; it was his duty to learn what it was. He slowly raised his roly-poly body on his short fluffy legs, lifted his little round head above the covering of his nest and peeped out into the woods. The sound had ceased as soon as he moved. He saw nothing, so took one step forward to a clear view, and instantly found himself face to face with an enormous Black Serpent. WILD ANIMALS I HAVE KNOWN, 1898

Seton shows the snowshoe rabbit, or varying hare, walking in his brown summer coat. Seton often sketched the animal, known as "the bread of the woods"—the prey of many furred predators and rapacious birds.

Mink

The Weasel is a sanguinary little incarnation of fury and valour, with but little cunning; it is low in intelligence and incapable of friendship with man or anyone else. The Otter, though a Weasel in pedigree, seems to have responded to the elevating and gentling influences attendant on the fisher-life. It is the least destructive, the most docile and intelligent of the Family. The Mink is half-way between in habits and character, as it is in food and haunts. After sojourning in the reeds along the river for a time catching fish and killing Muskrats in Otter-fashion, or running down Rabbits and Mice Weasel-fashion, it may set out across country to find better hunting and happen, in its travels, to discover the real Happy Hunting Ground in the form of some farmer's barnyard. Very naturally, it settles down in this ideal spot—didn't it set out to find this very thing?—this highly populated wilderness of buildings and sheltered nooks is perfect and here "every prospect pleases—only man is vile." The Mink's attitude toward this game preserve is quite different from that of the lesser Weasels. *They* are mad to kill—kill—kill; they will, if possible, kill everything there in one night, then leave the ruined place to seek some new field of carnage. Not so the Mink. It has but little of the killer spirit. It kills because it must eat, and, having found the well-stocked henneries, it says to itself, "Here now will I settle down, eat, drink, and make merry, for these are mine own preserves by right of discovery, and I will defend them against all invaders." On the list of invaders it puts the farmer and his family, and his dogs and his cats, and all those that put their trust in him. From safe hiding under the barn or in the log-pile it sallies forth at night to kill and eat; sometimes one fowl each night for many nights in succession; sometimes it yields to the blood-lust (not unknown among mankind), and kills half a dozen of the defenseless prey, feasting only on those choicest parts of all, the blood and brains, just as the Buffalo killer would shoot down half a dozen Buffalo because it was so easily possible, and then take nothing but the tongues.

Usually the Mink is killed before leaving the barnyard precincts, but it often happens that a number of narrow escapes from shot-guns or dogs decide it to move on. In the hours of the night it goes forth, bounding with high-arched back. Its speed is not great, but, like all Weasels, it is possessed of endless strength and doggedness, and though a man can outrun it on the open and outwalk it travelling, its steady bounding may take it miles away before morning. As it journeys it is ever on the alert for guidance from its nose. There are a thousand accidents to turn its steps one way or another; the cluck of a grouse, the rustle of a Mouse in the grass, an easier path, a promising odour in the wind, the wind itself, may each and all give trend to its tireless bounding and bring the hunter at last to some marsh-land of promise, or mayhap another barnyard, wherein it may settle down again to comfort of a kind, taking, undoubtedly, its life in its teeth while doing so, a condition that it has not the wit to think about, and if it had it would simply dismiss the thought, viewing this merely as a normal condition of all existence. The Mink certainly never spent a moment of its life without being under the shadow of impending death, and as certainly it never lost a wink of sleep through thinking about it.

If surprised during its hunting or suddenly brought face to face with man, it often rises up on its hind-quarters to get a better view; in this position it looks extraordinarily long. I once met one out on the prairie. It rose up to scan me from every one of its twenty-four inches of stature, and stood so till I came within ten feet and removed the top of its head with a thimbleful of sparrow-shot.

The species is active and hunts chiefly by night, but is often seen in the daytime, especially in the mating season and in the fall. LIFE HISTORIES OF NORTHERN ANIMALS, 1909

Beaver

Like most of the rodents which do not hibernate, the Beavers store up food for winter. All through the autumn they labor; the suitable trees next the bank are first attacked; if they fall into the water they are allowed to lie there, as it is easy to cut their branches later under the ice. If they fall on the land all the branches are cut off into pieces of a size possible to handle, that is to say, "when 5 inches in diameter they are usually about a foot long, when 4 inches in diameter they are about a foot and a half long, and when 3 inches in diameter are about 2 feet long. Poles from 1 to 2 inches in diameter are often found 8, 10 or 12 feet in length, and also cut up into short lengths from a few feet to a few inches long." They are brought to the lodge to be stored in two different ways. The heavier timbers are sunken in the bottom of the pond. How they are sunken is often discussed. I have heard men who should have known better say that the Beaver sucks all the air out of them to make them sink, or that the Beavers charm them and at your touch the charm is broken, they float up. The fact is that most green woods are nearly as heavy as water. If waterlogged they are heavier. The Beaver carries the green stick down to the bottom and partly buries it in the mud; very little holds it. In a week or so it is waterlogged and lies there even if uncovered. If any one pulls at a piece of poplar, for example, just after it is sunken, it floats and will not stay down without weighting. These things I saw and proved to my own satisfaction on the Nyarling River, near Great Slave Lake, in June, 1907. LIFE HISTORIES OF NORTHERN ANIMALS, 1909

Woodchuck

I n my early days about Lindsay, Ontario, the Woodchuck was the largest wild animal that entered into the lives of us boys. In the grain fields, still dotted with stumps, it found a homeland very much to its taste. With some great stump to stand guard over its doorway, its roots for posts to block all ruthless digging foes, its top to furnish a sunning place and observatory, each fat, contented Woodchuck lives— the happy lord of the small domain about its door. At times, though rarely, the long rifle of the grown-ups would end the càreer of some rack-renting Chuck that wasted by overtaxing its little manor; or perhaps the Fox, who prowled early, snapped up the Woodchuck that prowled late. But upon the whole it had little to fear from any but the boys and their ever-

The woodchuck, never too far away from one of his den entrances, surveys the scene for intruders.

present auxiliary, the house dog. Many times, as I now recall with over-long delayed remorse, we played a boyish, fiendish part. That same old dog, by cutting off some Chuck afield from its fortress, would drive it into a treacherous hollow log or burrow just begun. Here it needs must turn to fight—for the Woodchuck, though wisely ready ever to retreat if possible, will *never surrender*. No, it is a fighter, and fight it will, with the courage of a hero, both dogs and boys innumerable; whistling its shrill alarm, desperately grating its teeth till their splinters fly, seizing on anything, dog or stick, that comes in reach; defying all, till the brutal twisting-stick entangled in its fur gives it the unexpected jerk that throws it on the mercy of foes that know no mercy; a scuffle then—a crunching of bones—and the Red Monk's life has ended in a tragedy.

But these were individual cases. The race is far indeed from ending. In those, that now I call my Woodchuck days, the Bear, the Deer, the Beaver, the Wolf, and even the Porcupine were gone, but the Woodchuck throve, as still it does. Without the cunning, the speed, the strength, the armament, or the prowess of any of these, it still has a secret better than all that gifts it with power to hold its own. The secret of its life and the sum of its wisdom is this—keep close to the ground. In time of fear it flies to Mother Earth. This, indeed, is wisdom, for our wise men tell us all flesh is earthborn Anteus-like, that nations die as surely as they quit the soil. Here man himself might learn a lesson; while others pass away, the Woodchuck's race yet lives and thrives and holds its ancient range. LIFE HISTORIES OF NORTHERN ANIMALS, 1909

Raccoon

This is strictly nocturnal if any animal ever is; the darkest hours of night are its favorite time for prowling, which, nevertheless, does not prevent enterprising reformers of the race occasionally setting forth on a diurnal excursion, for which they not uncommonly share the fate of unnumbered reformers, and win, without wearing, a martyr's crown.

Although nesting and resting in trees, where it moves about with slow caution of 'Possum and Bear, rather than the reckless agility of Marten and Squirrel, the Coon travels, hunts, and feeds almost exclusively on the ground.

It may occasionally rob the nest of woodpecker, Squirrel, or other tree-dweller, but such must not be considered its normal habit of life—by far the greatest bulk of its food is taken on or near the ground.

In a wild state, the summer-long main support of the Coon is frogs. In catching them by night it is singularly expert, and when the frog takes refuge in the muddy bottom, the Coon, with wonderfully dextrous, tactile fingers, gropes after it. Leaving the enterprise entirely to its paws, its eyes may scan the woods and shores in a vacant way, but its mind is in touch with the finger-tips; and the frog that escapes them must indeed be worthy to live and father a superior race. LIFE HISTORIES OF NORTHERN ANIMALS, 1909

Muskrat

The diagram represents a Muskrat's home that I examined at Cos Cob, Conn., in July, 1905. It was under a clump of young ash trees and presents all the usual characteristics of the bank dens. Nos. 2 and 3 were holes at water level. They were plugged up with grass and sticks as when exposed by the water lowering; 1, the real entrance, was deep under water and was made later; 5 was a den with about 2 inches of water in it; 6, a small den not connected with the others; 7, a small den at a lower level than the main den; at 9 is a plunge hole from the den into deep water; 8 was the main den, nearly round, 15 inches each way, smoothed with great labor in gnawing off thick roots. It was very near the surface and had a ventilator under the stick pile, as also had 6. The pathways were evidently made by the Muskrats in carrying up these sticks.

The main den had quantities of green grass and stalks in the corners; among these jewel-weed was prominent. This was fresh cut, and may have been either food or bedding, probably both.

This den illustrates the style of all those I have examined on

Sunning

mastology

Coon left hind (dry)

Indian Pipe
Scioto . O.
photo by
H. Bannon

inches

Forest & Stream

left front

(dry)

Raccoon exploring Crawfish hole

Anyone who has watched a wild raccoon cannot help but be fascinated by the almost human way it uses its forepaws. The Indian artist who created the pipe noted this too.

banks. They have one main entrance under water, sometimes other smaller entrances. The tunnel leads up to a commodious den, which is open to the air at one small place, and covered outside with a pile of sticks and grass.

The main features of this agree perfectly with those of the nest made in a rat-house. The stick pile over the roof shows how easily one grades into the other.

There was no dung anywhere in the dens; all was sweet and clean.   LIFE HISTORIES OF NORTHERN ANIMALS, 1909

Opossum

There are three essentials to make a Possum paradise —foods, woods, and water. All its far-flung searching parties have followed the rivers through more or less timber. Where the timber ceases, or the water ends, the Possum halts its onward march.

Rocky uplands are not to its taste, but a swamp it loves; and where there are hollow trees near by for lodging, the Possum is content to take a chance on the food question.

Hundreds of men have spent their lives in Possum country, and yet have never seen a live, loose Possum. The creature is so strictly nocturnal, and so secretive, that it is seldom found till trapped, or else treed by some night-roving Dog.

So far as recorded, the Possum is one of the most silent of our animals. It has no call note, no note of recognition or of anger, except at rare times a low growl; or occasionally a faint hissing, when, with mouth wide open, it views the approach of a stranger.

Nevertheless all this is but the casual and superficial observation of persons who have had but fleeting glimpses of the creature under circumstances when its evident policy was to keep quiet. Some day our younger and more minutely observant naturalists will tell us of its extensive list of sounds, with calls to mate or young ones—yes, even a love-song for the love-time. Has it not vocal apparatus and strongly marked instincts and desires that need expression?

LIVES OF GAME ANIMALS, 1925–1927

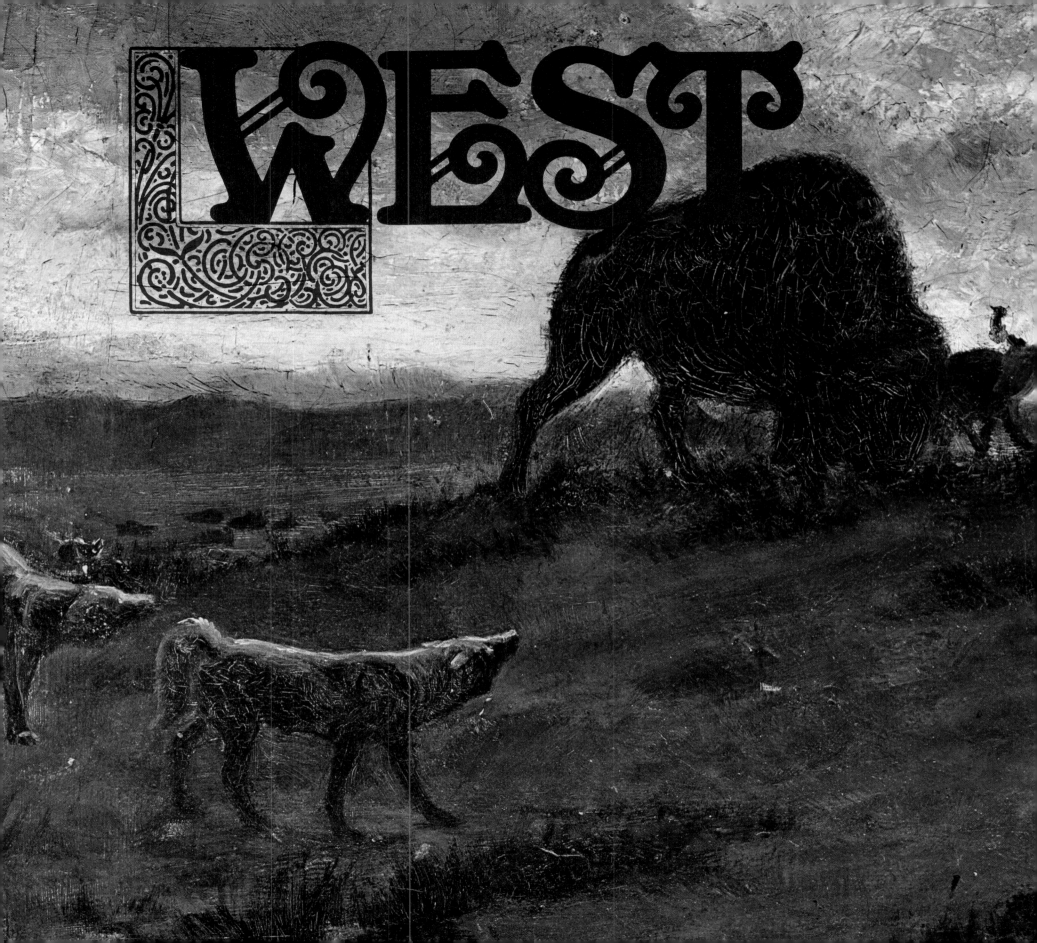

WEST

Even to one used to the vastness of the Canadian prairies the Rockies were an incredible sight, from the towering, snow-blanketed reaches of the Pacific Northwest to the last tapering, sun-scorched pinnacles of the Guadalupe Range near the Texas border in southern New Mexico.

There was the feeling of the immensity of the peaks as the train strained—its multiple steam engines puffing like laboring oxen—across Raton Pass in southern Colorado in the 1890's. Coming west to trap wolves had been an impulse thing, but it would be the introduction to a part of the West which remained deeply etched in memory. After the grime and crowds of New York and Chicago, the second impression of the land, after vastness, was one of cleanness—wind-washed and sun-baked, bleached clean by the elements. And yet, mixed with the newness of the West and contrasted with the feeling of decay in the major cities of the East, there was the sense of antiquity. Mountains, upended millions of years earlier by gigantic forces—which shoved, wrenched, and twisted the rock formations of long-dead oceans—bared their story to the eyes of all. Sheer cliffs of tans, ochres, reds, and purples—layer upon layer of sandstone and shale—spread the geologic history of ages beneath the glaring sunlight, and one became small and insignificant before the record. For in all the hundreds of vertical feet of geologic time, the recorded history of mankind might represent no more than a line the thickness of a piece of writing paper.

The furrowed, piñon- and juniper-clad foothills of northeast New Mexico, where the wolves were wreaking havoc with the cattle herds, stretched gradually to the grassy plains farther south. There the gently rolling land was spotted with towns formed along the Santa Fe Trail, which started in Independence, Missouri, and snaked its way westward, finally reaching Santa Fe. There were towns named Wagon Mound, Clayton, Moses, Springer, Watrous, and Colmor. Dusty trails, boarded towns with narrow streets, bearded men and plank sidewalks, horses, buckboards, mules, oxen, and cowboys—tanned, leathery old-timers, open-faced youngsters in bib overalls, and Mexican vaqueros with wide-brimmed hats—saloons, rooming houses, and barbed-wire fences stretched as far as the eye could see. And over it all burned the sun, a constant orb in the incredible cleanliness of the sky. There were the days of wind—with blasts hurtling down the narrow main streets of small towns, driving clouds of dust against weathered walls and corral fences and piling the bouncing tumbleweeds against wire fences on both sides of narrow, rutted roads. Violent blizzards whipped across the rolling plains as late as May—driving cattle and horses before them until the animals fell, ice coating their nostrils and mouths to the point where they suffocated or simply died from the sub-zero cold.

And there were the still days of spring when the Harris hawks and golden eagles circled gently high above, and the far-off peaks stood white against the sky—their slopes covered with ponderosa pine and blue spruce. The hundreds of thousands of prairie dogs, clustered in their "towns" across the plains, barked at the passing rider and then dove into their holes at the last moment. Food for the weasel, the desert fox, the golden eagle, the red-tailed or rough-legged hawk, the prairie falcon, the coyote, and the desert owls, these stub-tailed rodents were hated by the cowboys because their dens caused so many horses to step into them and break a leg. Pronghorn herds browsed in the shallow, grass-lined valleys and seldom fled unless approached rapidly or shot at. But when pursued they would streak single-file across the ridges with a flat, fluid-looking running style more like that of a dog or wolf than a hoofed animal. The meat was good to eat if one shot a young animal before flight, as it stood looking at the hunter with that strange curiosity common to the animal. If the animal was killed after running any distance, the adrenaline secreted in its attempt to escape changed the taste of the meat and it was far more gamy.

The gray prairie wolves, the lean red wolves up from the border of Mexico, and the occasional southward-roaming timber wolves down from the peaks of the high country were everywhere. Scourge of the ranchers and sheepmen, they killed and fed upon cattle, horses, sheep, goats, and swine alike. What the wolves failed to kill, the coyotes and desert foxes and bobcats did. A rancher was beset with frustration when the big wolves became thick on his range land, but the Mexican sheepherder fared little better as he tried to safeguard his flocks in the hills near the small adobe towns. While the rancher had his rifle and side arm in case of an occasional sighting, the sheep rancher had little but his sheep dogs to try and frighten away the marauder, and while they might outbluff the coyote, bobcat, and even the occasional young mountain lion, they were no match for the wolves.

The efforts to trap the wolves led to endless days in the saddle and countless nights spent boiling traps, smoking clothing, and repairing poison baits. Each defeat, though agonizing, became a personal challenge. And at first there was only defeat after defeat as the wily wolves eluded each careful set. But finally, with the help of a few expert trappers, there were those sets that worked. It was these experiences that inspired the books of Lobo and Blanca, and while a lifelong distaste for the steel-jawed leg trap developed, there also remained a lifelong memory of the strength, cunning, and ferocity of the wolf itself. No man who has seen what wolves can do to a pregnant cow or mare could have

LOCO-WEED

any doubt that nature is cruel. The partly eaten bodies of these animals, with not much more than the fetus consumed before the pack departed, remain in memory a long time. And a wolf dies as it lives, defiant to the end, as it should in its world.

Between trapping sorties there was time to travel to the high country, where, once the spring runoff of deep snow had poured down the thousands of streams from the snowpack region near and above the timberline, fragile mountain flowers grew beside tiny clear streams in the high valleys and the thin clean air carried the scent of pine, spruce, and the damp-earth smell of meadows formed from long-abandoned beaver ponds. One would occasionally come upon a vacant cabin occupied, decades before, by a trapper and mountain man who had spent months in these high valleys gathering furs to trade at the base of the Sangre de Cristo range, the Taos Mountains, and in the adobe-house cities of Santa Fe and Taos.

High on the rocky talus slopes scurried the whistling marmots and pikas, while farther down the horses would surprise golden-mantled ground squirrels, the tassel-eared squirrel, the small red squirrel or chickaree, and the tiny, nervous, and jerky chipmunk. At stops the black-and-white whiskey-jack camp jays would steal the crust of bread from between fingers if one turned a head, and small native trout flashed upstream and beneath banks of small streams as the horses lowered their heads to drink. At altitudes above 9,000 feet the heart would pound in the chest after walking. And now and then there would be the heart-pounding thrill of coming upon the huge grizzly—perhaps caught in the act of smashing a rotting log to bits in search of grubs, or feeding on the berry patches on a high slope. The horses knew the bear and would tend to bolt at the first scent, but the big bears, if not challenged, usually went their own way. The smaller black bears would run at the first sight of man, as did the magnificent bull elk, surprised browsing in some lonely park near the edge of the spruce timber. And it was always with wonder that one watched a herd of bulls, cows, and calves pass through the dense, blow-down spruce falls without making a sound or slowing the even strides. Now and then, through binoculars, one caught sight of the bighorn sheep, but usually only up on the rocky outcroppings or lying on a patch of sunlit slope far above the timberline. The big mule deer were everywhere, from the foothills to the high peaks, and the large bucks sported magnificent antlers. Their bounding flight—soundless and sure-footed as a mountain goat—was a constant source of joy to watch. One day there was the discovery of a great-horned owl nest in a conifer at the head of a narrow valley. In it were two white, downy chicks, plump and well fed on a diet of squirrels, pine martens, mice, and spruce grouse. That night the *hoo, hoo, hoo . . . hoo, hoo* of the owls floated on the calm mountain air as flames from the ponderosa logs flickered against the spruce trunks. There was the track of a mountain lion, fresh in the black mud on the bank of a stream crossing, but never a sight of the big, tawny cat—nor ever a sight of that elusive predator in the wilds.

But that was only the first voyage to the Rockies, and there were to be many in the years to come—the great land beckoning with its siren call as it has to so many men for so many hundreds of years. There was camping in Montana and Wyoming, and there were the wonders of Yellowstone and the land of the sulfur springs and geysers. The dall sheep and the white goats of the Pacific Northwest remained deep in memory. The black and white of magpies in Colorado, gliding in their peculiar flight from willow to cottonwood along the streams, was as much a part of the West as the Black Hills of South Dakota, where the remnants of the Nez Percé evaded the last of the pursuing U.S. Cavalry in the swirling snow. The West was also the rain forests of the Pacific North-

west, where the bald eagles perched on the dead limbs waiting for the spent salmon to wash up on a gravel bar, and the black-tail deer of the Sierras of Southern California.

But above all it was New Mexico, a curious blend of all the best, that stayed with a man from that first trip in the 1890's. It was that same ancient, yet always-new land that called whenever the East became too crowded, when the mind became weary or the soul in need of refreshing. It was that land that called as no other place. And when the auto became more sophisticated, it was there that exploring became a thing of great pleasure for a man to whom long-distance walking was a thing of the past.

The towering Rockies of Montana and Wyoming and Colorado were one aspect of the great mountain ridge that runs down the spine of North America. The other was the last of the Rockies that extend from the southern border of Colorado to the Texas line east of El Paso. On both sides of the Rio Grande—from where it enters New Mexico on the north as a clear, wide, trout-filled stream at the bottom of a 1,000-foot-deep gorge, to where it passes El Paso as a sluggish, muddy river—rises a series of mountain ranges. The heavily forested Taos Mountains in whose peaks nestle clear lakes—the Latir Lakes, Heart Lake, Lost Lake—gradually give way to the Sangre de Cristo Range. Towering above Santa Fe, they contain other timberline lakes—Pecos Baldy Lake, Spirit Lake, Lake Katherine, and the headwaters of the Pecos River. There were the trips in the fall high into this country where the aspens flamed golden against the blue-green spruce and beaver hurried to complete the underwater pile of birch, aspen, and willow limbs before sub-zero nights in late September skimmed the ponds with ice.

And no single night remained more etched in the memory of a life than one spent driving up the meandering curves of La Bajada Hill on the way from Albuquer-

---

The shrike, or butcherbird, is a small predator. It kills and eats insects (especially grasshoppers), snakes, and lizards—sometimes impaling them for storage on points of barbed wire.

que in a heavy snowstorm in December. Decades later there was still the clear picture of the almost-obscured roads, the driving snow, and the headlights of other cars as the outskirts of Santa Fe came into view. And as the car finally inched into the plaza of Santa Fe, across from the ancient adobe walls of the Palace of the Governors and to the brightly lit doorway of the La Fonda, there was no sound as the tires rolled on inches of newly fallen snow. A Pueblo Indian, heavily robed, squatted in the lighted doorway—silver jewelry spread over a brightly colored blanket on the flagstone floor in front of him. Across the plaza came the sounds of Mexican music from a café and over the entire scene floated the scent of burning piñon logs from the hundreds of adobe chimneys in the ancient city, which was already a territorial capital and a seat of Spanish government when the first Pilgrims landed at Plymouth Rock.

And the chain of mountain ranges kinked its way southward—the mighty Jemez Range to the west of the huge river, where it ran between moderately high mesa walls near the pueblo of the Cochiti tribe and then glided, bulging full in spring and meandering small in the summer months, past the stately Sandia Mountains. Prairie falcons and barn owls nested on the sheer walls of the mesa cliffs south of Cochiti, and the brown waters of the Rio Grande were turned a reddish color as the waters of the Jemez River entered it north of Bernalillo.

From Bernalillo south, the fertile farmlands of the valley spread from mesa to mountain foothills—the rich loam of the valley floor bringing forth the miles of apple, peach, plum, and cherry trees, along with verdant fields of corn and chili, and truck gardens rich with lettuce, tomatoes, and beans. Red foxes and their gray cousins prowled the river bottoms—preying on the warrens of cottontail rabbits, gray squirrels, and mice infesting the damp land beneath ancient cottonwoods and thick growths of willow, tamarisk, and Russian olive bushes.

Skunks, bobcats, and coyotes added to the predator population as did the myriad of hawks and great-horned owls. Bank beaver were a constant source of annoyance to the native Spanish farmer—digging into irrigation ditches and spilling precious irrigation waters from the mother ditch, or acequia madre, before it could be diverted into the thirsty farmland. Hordes of mourning doves nested in the orchards as the spring blossoms turned the barren valley into a sea of color each spring, and the evening sky was filled with the thunder of the nighthawk call as it vied with bats for the hosts of insects.

South of the fault-block range of the Sandias, the knife-edged Manzanos fell off abruptly from the gradual rise leading westward from the Estancia Valley; the sheer 4,000-to-5,000-foot drop left one breathless if viewed from the top. Below, the mighty river flowed in its endless curves, wending southward between ever-lower but still massive mountain ranges to the east and west of its banks—the Magdalena Range to the west, the Black Range, home of the feared Chiricahua Apaches, south and west of that; to the east of the river the arid and mountain-mahogany-covered San Andres Mountains, bordering the vast gypsum desert known to the early Spanish Conquistadors as the Jornada del Muerto, or the "journey of death." The Mescalero Apaches lived in their ancestral home to the east of the white sands, safe from any attack in their White Mountain stronghold—from which they had for decades preyed upon wagon trains and U.S. Cavalry intrepid enough to seek them out from forts along the river—even now bleached ruins in the desert: Fort Selden and Fort Fillmore. Many a cavalryman's bones lay beneath the white sands after crossing through San Augustin Pass in more than one futile attempt to prevent the Mescaleros from killing early Spanish settlers in towns along the Rio Grande, one of which was named Las Cruces . . . for the crosses studding the valley bottom.

Rocky Mountain bighorn, the largest of the North American wild sheep.

And in this land the sidewinder wriggled unmolested in the scorching sun and the whip scorpion and lithe, amber centipede were preyed upon only by the shrike and the precocious roadrunner. Here the badger held sway in the hot earth and the herds of javelina feasted upon the prickly pear and yucca as the sun set in a molten sky to the west each day. Desert mule deer and the dainty whitetail deer fed on cactus blossoms and buckbrush buds, and here the mourning and white-wing doves nested on the prairie earth—so numerous that not even the burrowing owls, weasels, and coyotes made a dent in the daily population of their millions. Here the coatamundi and the armadillo roamed the arroyo bottoms and flocks of Merriam turkeys fed on the weed seeds of foothills in the years before they were driven into the high mountains by the gradual encroachment of ranchers and farmers. The desert bighorn sheep dwelled then in the Florida Mountains, on the sheer peaks of the majestic Organ Mountains, and on the barren slopes of the Hatchet Mountains, baking on the flat desert plain just before the Territory ended at the border of Mexico. Red wolves crossed the shallow river after dark and made their way north through the Mogollon Mountains and the Black Range until they spilled out upon the lava flats south of the vast Navajo lands. There they slaughtered the Navajo sheep, helped by the gray prairie wolves and the coyotes, and were stopped by no one. Other wolves moved up from the Sierra Madre Range of Chihuahua and migrated—along with the lean mountain lion—from the tip of the Guadalupe Range south of the White Mountains until they overflowed into the Pecos Valley to the east and found vast herds of white-faced Herefords upon which to prey nightly. And in that land of alkali flats—with places named Gut Ache Mesa, Slaughter Canyon, Antelope Sink, Diamond Mound, Laguna Plata, and High Lonesome, and towns named Hagerman and Loving and Whites City—did the wolves feed on fat cattle and sheep.

To the north—for half a thousand miles, following the great Pecos River and finally into the rugged breaks of the Canadian River—roamed the endless herds of antelope, and during the spring could be heard the booming of prairie chickens. In the fields of broom corn, stretching to the horizon, the entire continental population of sandhill cranes wintered, filling the skies with the strings of their flights and the querulous croaking rattle of their calls. In the darkness the barn owls, burrowing owls, and short-eared owls flitted across the grassy plains bordering the mighty Pecos River, and huge tarantulas reflected auto headlights on the dusty roads—eyes ruby-red and staring as the hairy spiders, the size of coffee saucers, rose and fell on spindly legs.

And the same land rolled farther north until, again, it became one with the beginning of the foothills at the base of the Santa Fe Trail and the piñon and juniper replaced the grass. Almost half a century afterward—as the burnished sun slipped behind the western horizon—one could see the deep ruts of the wide trail which had carried west so many hopes and dreams, and had seen the deaths of many of these same hopes and dreams. For the Trail was not then, nor is it today, a narrow thing—such as a road or highway. It was a great land river, miles wide, over which moved the hundreds of thousands of pioneers seeking new life and a new beginning. Past towns named Cimarron and Maxwell and Rowe, Glorieta and Cañoncito, moved the vast fleet of wagons—leaving behind, for generations to see, the ruts etched into the face of a nation. And over those same ruts today flit the marsh hawk by day and the desert owls by night—both on their endless hunt for rodents. And as the sun leaves the western sky a glory of gold each sunset, the coyotes start their evening songs as they did millions of years ago—when they and the prairie wolves owned this land. . . .

JOHN G. SAMSON

The elegant speedster, the pronghorn, in all its positions and all its moods permeates Seton's West.

Gray Wolf, Peccary, Buffalo, Bighorn, White Sheep, Pronghorn, Elk, Cougar, Franklin's Ground Squirrel, Chickaree, Bobcat, Prairie Hare, Jack Rabbit, Snowshoe Rabbit, Rockchuck, Wolf, Mule Deer, Marmot, Blacktail Deer, Eyra Cat, Armadillo, Ocelot, Kangaroo Rat, White Goat, Coyote, Badger, Packrat, Prairie Dog, Weasel

Lobo

So, on January 4, 1894, I set out for the Currumpaw, taking over a hundred big steel traps, the wagon and team, and two helpers, Billy Allen and Charley Winn. On arrival, we prepared the old Currumpaw ranch house for a prolonged stay, and began a methodic exploration of the country.

Very soon, I learned that the cowmen of the Currumpaw believed the wolf bands to be led by an immensely big strong wolf of supernatural cunning.

My great problem was to get this notorious wolf, the "Lobo of Currumpaw." In my book, *Wild Animals I Have Known,* I give the story at length; but in my lectures I have adopted the briefer form, the one given here.

To understand his nature, one must remember that a wolf is nothing but a big wild dog getting his living by his wits, his speed, and the strength of his jaws.

If a wolf pup be taken very young, and brought up in the ranch, he behaves much like a dog. Some, at least, so taken, are perfectly kind and friendly.

But Lobo, the big wolf of Currumpaw, was not brought up in this fashion. He brought himself up, not indoors, but out on the open range; and he was far from being as kind as a dog. He was a bad old cattle-killer. It was commonly said that he killed a cow every night, which may or may not be true. Of course, he did not need that much meat. But the belief was that his devilish cunning warned him never to return to his kill; it was too apt to be surrounded by traps and poison the day after the killing. Therefore, fresh beef every night was his rule. Coyotes, or who would, might feast on the leavings.

At the very outset, I found I could not shoot this wolf with a long-range rifle, for the very simple reason that I never saw him. He knew that men carry guns—against guns he could do nothing. He hid all day up in the hills, somewhere, we never knew where. But night-time he would come. And we could always tell when he was about by his voice. A common gray wolf makes a howl like *ow-w-ow.* But the howl of the big wolf was more like *Ow-ow-ow,* an octave lower; and whenever that came booming down the canyon, one of the boys would say: "There he is; I'd know that howl anywhere. That's old Lobo."

We could, if we chose, go to the door of the cabin, and shoot off a gun in the direction of the howl—and maybe hit some old cow. The wolf cleared out—he would not face the guns. But he would come back later, or to some other part, and get whatever he wanted—that is, our best beef.

I was soon satisfied that guns were no use to us in this hunt, so I set to work with poison. The boys said, scornfully: "Poison! Bah! He knows more about poison than you do. He won't take a poison bait, nor let any other wolf take one. We've tried every way."

I thought I had some new devices. It took me a month to be convinced that I could not kill him with poison. He merely served the baits with a wolf's contempt; and the fact that it was his doing was plainly recorded by his immense track, a third bigger than that of any other wolf.

The total failure of the poison left me with but one more stratagem, that is, steel traps. I got out my hundred heavy double-spring steel wolf-traps, and set them with great care in all the trails leading to the watering-places, and the canyon crossings.

I know how to trap. The traps and chains were rubbed with fresh blood, also my boots and leather gloves. I touched nothing with naked hands. Each trap was fastened by a stout chain to a short log. The traps were buried in the dust of the trail, the logs on each side of the trail—four traps about a foot apart. When all was perfectly concealed, with dust and grass put back as it had been, I took the body of a rabbit; and with this, smoothed out every sign of disturbance. No man could tell that there were traps hidden in that dust. The cattle could not tell. Our dog could not tell; he would blunder into them in broad daylight. We had to take him out again and again. He

was none the worse; for the traps have no teeth, they merely hold firmly.

The dog could not sense the danger, nor the cattle, nor the men; but that old wolf did.

When he got to A, he stopped. His keen nose, no doubt, warned him that there was something suspicious ahead. He began very cautiously to scratch. By chance, he discovered the chain at B. Now he knew *where* the trap was, as well as *what* it was. He scratched all along, exposed the trap, turned it upside down—then went on and killed a thoroughbred Hereford cow.

This sort of thing he did many times. But I noticed at length that when he got to A, his first move was to stop, try the wind, then move off the trail to the down-wind side.

That gave me a new idea. I set three traps on each side of the trail; then, in the middle, one trap, forming an "H." Now, I thought, he will come down the trail to C. There his nose will warn him; he will turn aside down-wind, and certainly get into one of the side traps. It could not fail.

He came that second night. He cautiously wandered down—down—till he got to C. Then what warned him I do not know; but, instead of abruptly leaving the trail there, he *backed out* on his own tracks till quite beyond the dangerous ground. Then from one side, he scratched sticks and stones with his hind feet, dog-fashion. He sent them flying over the traps, till all were exposed and sprung—and went on to kill another valuable cow.

I was at my wits' end now. I had been in pursuit of him, not two weeks, as I had expected, but four months; and I was no nearer to success than any other man. Yes, the old wolf might have been there yet, but that he made one terrible mistake. Oh! be warned by his blunder. He married a very young and very silly wife.

All this time I never saw the wolves. But the Mexican shepherds did. These men were out all night with their flocks; and many times in the dim light of their watchfires, the shepherds saw the grim wolves sneaking around. . . .

Two prairie wolves prowl carefully about a newborn buffalo calf —safe as long as the cow is there to protect it. Soon, even within hours, the shaky-legged calf will be able to outrun its enemies in a fair chase.

So, early the second morning, I went up to the North Canyon. And sure enough, when I got to the place of the traps, here, lying in them was Old Lobo, the King Wolf. He had struck the trail that I had made with Blanca's paw. He thought it was her trail, that she was just on ahead, he would soon find her now.

He had followed it recklessly, and had fallen into all four traps. There he lay, a trap on each foot, the chains all tangled together. Perfectly helpless he was; and round about at a safe distance were the cattle, bellowing, tossing up the dust, to insult the fallen despot. But they did not dare to go near him.

When he saw me coming, he raised his voice in the muster call of the pack, signalling, "Come on now." He made that canyon reverberate for the last time; and for the first time in his life, I suppose, there were none who answered—no one to come at his call.

Then, left alone in his extremity, all he wanted was to get at me, and die fighting. But he was held and helpless. When he fell to the ground, exhausted with this effort, I used my camera, and made the record that is given.

Then I took down my lasso; and as I did so something like pity possessed me. I had been after him for four months, the other men for five years; and now, when I found him in my power, I began to feel sorry for him.

"You grand old reprobate, you wonderful old hero. I am sorry for you. I am sorry to do it, but that's what I am here for."

I whirled my lasso; but just as the noose was dropping on his neck, he seized it in his jaws, and with one chop cut it in twain.

He looked at me, and seemed to say: "Now, try something else."

I had my gun; but, unwilling to use that, I rode back to camp, and got another lasso. Allen came with me this time. I flung a big stick to the wolf. In that, he saw only another enemy. He grabbed; then, before he could drop it, we both whirled our lassos. The nooses fell on his neck. The ponies know their business. In a few seconds, the light was nearly gone from those wonderful yellow eyes, when suddenly I shouted out: "No! No! Billy, not that! Slack up. We'll take him back alive."

He was quite helpless now. It was easy to put a big stick through his jaws, and a heavy cord around his muzzle. The stick kept the cord in, the cord kept the stick in. And once he found that his jaws were tied, his weapons gone, he made no more resistance. He never looked at me again; looked over me, past me, beyond me, behaved as though he were alone on the plains.

We fastened him securely, took him out of the traps, and laid him across my saddle. I on one side, Allen on the other, we brought him slowly back to the ranch house. . . .

There was no wound on his body, his eye was bright and clear, he seemed in perfect health that night when I went in and left him. But we know that an eagle robbed of his freedom, a lion shorn of his strength, a dove bereft of his mate, all die—they say, of a broken heart. And who will claim that that wild robber wolf could bear the threefold brunt, heartwhole?

This only I know: when the morning dawned, I stepped outdoors. He was lying just as I had left him, his head on his paws—his muzzle pointing down the canyon. But his spirit had flown—Old Lobo of the Currumpaw was dead.

I took the chain and collar from his neck, the cowboy came to help me. As we raised his body, there came from the near mesa, the long and mournful howling of the wolves. It may have been the ordinary hunting cry; but, coming at that moment, as it did, it seemed to me a long, sad, faraway farewell.

We carried the body into the outhouse, where lying still was the body of Blanca, his Blanca; and as we laid him down beside her, the cowboy said: "There, you *would* come to her, so now you are together again."

TRAIL OF AN ARTIST-NATURALIST, 1940

The badger, squat and robust though he is, is nevertheless a member of the weasel family. His great foreclaws enable him to dig out the labyrinthine burrows of the favorite prey, the prairie dog.

Now and then, through binoculars, one caught sight of the bighorn sheep, but usually only up on the rocky outcroppings or lying on a patch of sunlit slope far above the timberline. The big mule deer were everywhere, from the foothills to the high peaks, and the large bucks sported magnificent antlers. . . .

Bighorn ram, ewe, and lamb.

This unfinished sketch of a feeding bull elk nevertheless perfectly depicts the big animal as it browses on leaves and twig tips.

Gray Wolf

The range of the Gray-wolf has a known history. When the Buffalo swarmed over Western America from the Alleghenies to the Rockies, and from Great Slave Lake to Central Mexico, their herds were followed by troops of Buffalo-wolves that preyed on the weak and helpless. As the Buffalo disappeared the Wolves were harder put for a living. When the last great Buffalo herds were destroyed and the Wolves were left without their usual support, they naturally turned their attention to the cattle on the ranges.

The ranchmen declared vigorous war against them: traps and poison were imported in vast quantities, a bounty was offered for each Wolf scalp, and every inducement held out to wolf-hunters.

In those days the Wolves were comparatively unsuspicious, and it was easy to trap or poison them. The result was that enormous numbers were killed in the early days of 1880 to 1888 or 1889; so many, indeed, that the species seemed on the verge of extinction. The remnant of the race continued on the foothills of the Rockies or the Badlands, but they were so rare as to be no longer a factor in the cattle question. Then new knowledge, a better comprehension of modern dangers, seemed to spread among the Wolves. They learned how to detect and defy the traps and poison, and in some way the knowledge was passed from one to another, till all Wolves were fully possessed of the information. How this is done is not easy to say. It is easier to prove that it *is* done. Few Wolves ever get into a trap, fewer still get into a trap and out again, and thus learn that a steel-trap is a thing to be feared. And yet all Wolves have that knowledge, as every trapper knows, and since they could not get it at first-hand, they must have got it second-hand; that is, the information was communicated to them by others of their kind.

It is well known among hunters that a piece of iron is enough to protect any carcass from the wolves. If a Deer or Antelope has been shot and is to be left out over night, all that is needed for its protection is an old horseshoe, a spur, or even any parts of the hunter's dress. No Wolf will go near such suspicious-looking or human-tainted things; he will starve rather than approach the carcass so guarded.

With poison, a similar change has come about. Strychnine was considered infallible, when first it was introduced. It did vast destruction for a time, then the Wolves seemed to discover the danger associated with that particular smell, and will no longer take the poisoned bait, as I know from numberless experiences.

It is thoroughly well known among the cattle men now that the only chance of poisoning Wolves is in the late summer and early autumn, when the young are beginning to run with the mother. She cannot watch over all of them, the whole time, and there is a chance of some of them finding the bait and taking it before they have been taught to let that sort of smell-thing alone.

The result is that the Wolves are on the increase, have been, indeed, since the late 80's. They have returned to many of their old hunting-grounds in the cattle countries, and each year they seem to be more numerous and more widely spread, thanks to their mastery of the new problems forced upon them by civilization. LIFE HISTORIES OF NORTHERN ANIMALS, 1909

Peccary

The big boar is bossing the herd. His wisdom is not merely his own; but accumulated in his small brain is all the inherited wisdom of his forebears, manifested as guiding instincts. One of the elegant young lady-Pigs has been absent for some time. Each day she has been back for a spell—back in society. But the last day or two, she has been wholly out of sight till now. The herd has been rooting out vegetable delicacies, varied with grubs and beetles, and are nearly ready to head for the drinking place before settling for the noon sleep that every Muskhog takes during the heated hours—when back comes the lady-Pig; not alone this time, but followed by two funny little red roasters, not so big as Rabbits, but quick to run, and careful to stay right next to their mother.

The peccary, or wild pig of the Southwest deserts, is called a javelina in the U.S. Southwest and Mexico. Not a vicious animal, the pig at lower center is sketched yawning, a gentle mood in spite of the display of the formidable tusks —formidable, that is, to other peccary boars.

The old boar walks with slow dignity towards them—uttering an inquiring grunt. The mother faces him with mother-fortitude, and yet not without anxiety. The young ones dodge under her body. The big boar champs his teeth a little—very little—and slowly walking up, sniffs, sniffs. He is noting their smell—taking their fingerprints, as it were. And having sniffed, chopped his teeth, and yawned, he goes off. Others of the grown-ups sniff them too. Now the rusty twins have been admitted.

The whole troop heads for the water. There, under the cool palmettos, they lie sprawled till the afternoon is waning.

They are roused—by a whiff on the wind. Not a sound reaches them, but their sensitive nostrils bring notice that a great Cat—a Hunter-cat—is prowling near. With a little snort, the big boar springs to his feet, clicks the four bayonets in his mouth, and flings on the wind an intensified odour of musk. Everyone in the herd responds. The big boar leads the troop, and the sows line up. With manes erected they go, snorting, clicking their teeth, musking. With the recent mother and the two red Piglings in the middle rear, they march in a wide and threatening front to hunt that hostile smell. Soon they rout it out. He tried to hide in a low thicket, but the warrior Hogs are on him—and away dashes the Ocelot. He is swift, but his enemies are as quick, and are all about him before he knows it. In one short round, they will tear his velvet hide to tatters.

But the spotted hunter has a simple answer to their forces. He lightly springs up the nearest tree, and lies in open mockery as they swarm about and click their knives, or shrill their war cries, till they weary. The night comes on, and the Peccaries drift away to seek their evening meal.

LIVES OF GAME ANIMALS, 1925–1927

Buffalo

In 1882, when first I went to live in Western Manitoba, the prairie everywhere was dotted with old Buffalo skulls. Many had horns on them, but none had hair. Their condition and local tradition agree in fixing 1860 to 1865 as the epoch when the last Buffalo were killed on the Big Plain.

In the long slough east of Carberry I have found many Buffalo bones; and on August 13, 1899, I found a complete Buffalo skeleton there. No doubt, all the large bogs throughout Manitoba contain skeletons of Buffalo. . . .

There is on Antelope Island, in Salt Lake, a herd of Buffalo which numbered 28 in 1905. Friends in Salt Lake City have given me an idea of what has been going on in that herd, ever since they were turned loose and left free to resume their tribal life, a dozen years ago. The strongest bull takes possession of all the best things—the wallow, the choice food, the shady spot in summer, the sheltered nook in winter, and the majority of the cows. He would take all, if he had the wit, and the cows accepted his view of the matter. The lesser bulls keep out of his way and take what they can get of his leavings. From time to time, some growing lusty young fellow tries a bout with the "boss" and usually gets the worst of it. But a time comes, soon or late, when the "boss is licked." He is driven out of the herd and far away from it, forbidden to return at the peril of his life, and the new king reigns in his stead, to tyrannize over the cows and the lesser bulls as he did before. The reign of each "boss" is usually two or three years. I have no doubt that this explains the clan-life of the Buffalo. It is a well-known fact that any solitary Buffalo seen on the plains was always an outcast old bull—doubtless one that had been originally driven out of the herd, and, becoming indifferent to the other sex, remained more or less solitary from choice.

These old bulls are rarely molested by hunters, human or brute. They are too tough for one to eat or for the other to kill. But sometimes the Wolves, when hard pressed by hunger, will unite in a large band and attack even an old bull, if no better prey be in sight.

Fremont reckoned the annual market of Buffalo robes as 90,000; but robes were collected only during the four winter months, and not more than a third of those killed at the season were skinned, while half of the robes were used at home and never sent to market. Therefore, 90,000 robes represented a

Young bovines and deer appealed to Seton's imagination. This is evidently a bison calf, young enough to lack its later hump.

slaughter of about 1,920,000 Buffalo. But the rate of killing was so much higher in summer that we may calculate the annual kill at 2,000,000 or 2,500,000 a year during these palmy Buffalo days. The Buffalo Indians had been decreased by small-pox, but the white consumers more than made up the shortage. Naturally, therefore, the herds shrank fast.

In 1842 Fremont found distress among the Indians along the Platte on account of failure of the Buffalo. In 1852 the Buffalo was so far from the Red River country that Ross considered hunting it a thing of the past. In 1867 the Union Pacific Railway reached Cheyenne, penetrating the heart of the Buffalo country. It carried unnumbered destroyers with it and split the remaining Buffalo into halves. Thenceforth it was customary to speak of the "south herd" and the "north herd," each of which appeared to recognize a boundary in those sinister lines of steel.

In 1871 the Santa Fe Railway crossed Kansas, the favorite summer ground of the southern herd, now reduced to about 4,000,000, according to Hornaday. Then began the great slaughter by the white skin-hunters. Taking as a basis the railway statistics of shipments and Colonel Dodge's observations, Dr. Hornaday has calculated the slaughter of the herd as follows:

1872	*1,491,489*
1873	*1,508,658*
1874	*158,583*
Total	*3,158,730*
Killed by the Indians during the same period	*390,000*
Settlers and Indians........................	*150,000*
Total	*3,698,730*

These are the lowest estimates that I know of. Colonel Jones's figures are about double these. That was practically the end of the southern herd. A few scattered bands lingered in out-of-the-way places, but were relentlessly hunted down. The last considerable herd that I can learn about was in 1886,

described to me seven years afterward by Charles Norris, cowboy, of Clayton, N.M., whose narrative is full of interesting detail. The date seemed to me very late for so large a herd, but cross-examination did not make him change it.

The last big bunch of Buffalo he ever saw was in the "Panhandle" of Texas. He came on them in May of 1886. He was driving a bunch of horses from Coldwater to Buffalo Springs; and, when thirty-five miles east of Buffalo Springs, he saw the herd about three miles off, and knew at once they were Buffalo, because they were all of one color. He left the horses with the other man, as all he needed was a guide to this place. Next day, on returning, Norris saw the Buffalo again about fifteen miles farther east, and rode in among them. Some were lying down and some were grazing. They seemed about 200 in number; 6 only were little calves. As soon as they saw him they bunched like cattle and kept on "milling" around. Then one bull made a lead to stampede, but none followed him, so he came back to the bunch. Another bull then started from the bunch and tried to lead off. He ran about 100 yards, but none followed him at all, so he also returned to the bunch. Then one in the bunch that seemed a third larger than any other there led out and all following him, strung out in a semicircle. Norris tried to cut across to the middle of it; but instead of running right away, part of them hung back and it seemed as if they were going to surround him. He thought it wiser then to fall back and get out of the ring. Then they strung off after the big leader. Norris galloped behind trying to rope a calf, but the mother turned on him. He had no gun, and his horse was tired, so he gave it up. He noticed that in running they "pawed" with one side low, and after a while changed to the other. After they went off he rode on fifteen miles southeast to camp. A. N. Cranmer was in charge of the camp, which was by a small lake. He said: "This is the only water in this region and they will be certain to come in here before three days." So the men waited and on the second day, the whole herd appeared. Now they had a good chance to count them. There were 186. They drank very heavily and then played about like calves. A number of them amused themselves by jumping off a bluff into the water, four feet below them, then running around up a low place to jump off again. As soon as they had seen all they wished the men fired, killing a cow and a bull. They then set about roping some calves. Norris caught one and Cranmer caught two. They had to kill the mother of the last, as she showed fight. The herd went off and these men saw no more of it. One of the calves died and Norris gave his to Cranmer's little boy, who sold it to Goodnight, and the other was traded to a passing stranger from Kansas for a span of colts. In the November of the same year, on the same trail, Norris saw 12 head of Buffalo, but has never seen one since.

The very last individuals that I have knowledge of were found in 1889. The account of them I got from W. Allen, cowboy, also of Clayton, New Mexico, four years after the event. I give it in full.

About August 20, while out with a party hunting mustangs, in the neutral strip about twelve miles northeast of Buffalo Springs, the riders saw four animals, which they supposed were mustangs, as they were rolling in the dust. They were about three miles away, on the south side of a little knoll. The hunters rode around on the north side and got within seventy-five yards, to learn that these were four Buffalo.

They took alarm at once and started off westward, closely pursued by the hunters for about three miles, and then met another man driving a bunch of mustangs. The two bunches, mustangs and Buffalo, joined, and the men chased them for two miles, when they parted, the mustangs turning to the left, keeping up the XIT fence, and the Buffalo going to the right. Allen chased these about five miles farther and right into two of his own party. The Buffalo circled from them south and west three miles back, then right back to the XIT fence again. He fired four shots into a cow. She quit the bunch and went two miles to a lake, while he chased the three right through the XIT fence and left them. The men then returned to the cow at the lake; she ran into the deepest water, and stood at bay. After resting a short time she came out of the water and they shot

Falcons—seen over much of the West—were a favorite bird subject of Seton's.

her. A photographer, who was with the camp, took the pictures of the party with the skin and meat in view. That was the last Buffalo Allen ever saw. He learned that the three were killed later on.

This ended the last stragglers of the southern herd.

In 1878 the last great herd went south from the Saskatchewan, and the few scattered bands left behind were killed off by the Indians in 1879. In 1880 the Northern Pacific Railway opened a way into the central country of the last herd, and the southern story was repeated.

Condensing Dr. Hornaday's account we find that:

In 1881 hunters shipped out 50,000
In 1882 hunters shipped out 200,000
In 1883 hunters shipped out 40,000
In 1884 hunters shipped out 300
In 1885 hunters shipped out 0
Total 290,300

This was the end of the northern herd. The remnant, numbering perhaps 200 or 300, was scattered in droves among the Badlands between the Missouri and the Yellowstone. One of these bands, numbering 40 or 50, took refuge in the rough country along the Big Porcupine River, where 28 of them were killed in 1886 by Dr. Hornaday, who collected and afterwards mounted them for the United States National Museum.

The rest of these in the United States were soon picked off by cowboys and hunters.

Incompatible with any degree of possession by white men and with the higher productivity of the soil, therefore, he had to go. He may still exist in small herds in our parks and forest reserves. He may even achieve success as a domestic animal, filling the gaps where the old-time cattle fail. But the Buffalo of the wild Plains is gone forever; and we who see those times in the glamour of romance can only bow the head and sadly say, "It had to be. He served his time, but now his time is past."   LIFE HISTORIES OF NORTHERN ANIMALS, 1909

The recent presence of man, in this case Indians who with arrows have dispatched a horse, is sufficient to warn off carrion-minded coyotes until the man-smell is dissipated.

Bighorn

The marvellous curling horns of the rams were apparently the first things to catch the eyes, and rivet the attention of these early historians. Without exception, they comment on them.

The horns of the ram are the coveted trophy of the sportsman; for they are the creature's peculiar gift and crowning glory, his one distinguishing and imperishable ornament, the record of his size and of his life. . . . He must have been a noble animal, gifted at the outset with a robust constitution; or he could not have grown them so massive. To have outwitted his enemies long enough to have achieved that length, he must have been wise and crafty above his kind.

A horn that measures 36 in. around the outside curve, from base to tip, and 15 in. in girth at base, must be considered in the highest class.

The points of the Bighorn's horns are rarely entire; most have some inches missing. E. H. Ober maintains that this is caused by the horns being used to dig out roots among rocks, especially in seasons of drought, at which times in the Piute country, the sequaw root furnishes drink as well as food.

He says, further, that, as a consequence, "It is a very rare instance, indeed, to ever find a desert Nelson Sheep ram, in this locality, which has not the tip end of one or both of its horns broken; and it is an equally rare occurrence to find a Sierra Sheep with other than a perfect set of horns."

Charles Sheldon, however, does not accept this. He tells me that he is sure that it is the combat of the males that breaks the horn tips. They are splintered by the terrific jar, even when the tips themselves do not actually strike in the fight.

And it would surely be very unfair to the ewes if they could not dig up a drink, as well as the rams.

All the ancient records, and all the old-timers that I have consulted, tell that this creature was not originally a cliff-dweller. Its feeding grounds were the grassy foothills and bluffs not far from the crags. It would follow along the river bottoms to graze, but was ever ready to fly to the rocks for protection.

It was not gifted with speed, or weapons, or fighting strength; not could it find shelter underground like so many of the otherwise defenseless. But this it had—the power to bound up a sheer and rugged cliff that was impossible to any other big creature in its range—except, perhaps, a Cougar or a White Goat.

Today, all that is changed; the pressure of new perils has driven the Wild Sheep permanently to the high mountains. It is now a mountaineer. Nevertheless, it does, at times, set out across the level country to seek better forage. Its keen eye takes in mountains five to ten miles away; and the wise old ewe will strike out with her band, if she must, and make her way to the far, fair pastures she has spied out from some peak.

Some idea of the primitive number of Sheep may be formed from the population in Glacier National Park. In 1916, I spent some weeks camping in the Park, and after using all sources of information, calculated that the 2,500 square miles of the Park contained not less than 1,500 Sheep. In the official Report this estimate of mine was raised to 2,000, or about 1 Sheep to the square mile of this possible territory.

The Park is far from ideal range. It contains very little true Sheep pasture of the kind that they sought a hundred years ago. One can travel about a whole month, as I proved in 1916, and never see a Sheep. In the Big Horn Basin, judging by Lewis and Clark's accounts, and those of later travellers, Sheep may have been ten times as numerous as the above Park estimate. Offsetting this, however, is the sparse population of the arid desert regions. So that it is very safe to assume the primitive number at between 1,500,000 and 2,000,000. This, of course, does not include a Slim-horned Sheep of the north, whose numbers may be at least as great.

But even in the height of the love-and-war season, the ram seems to dispense with the unnecessary embellishment of loud talk. He looks at his enemy, shakes his head, maybe rears for a

The Rocky Mountain bighorn sheep became the hero of a book by Seton. The massive ram was named "Krag"—and possessed a set of horns that probably would have been a world record had they been real.

moment. The other knows exactly what that means, and gets ready. They back off a little for a good start, and from a hundred feet apart, they let loose. With a muzzle velocity of 20 miles an hour, they meet like two pile-drivers. The crack of horn against horn can be heard two miles off on a calm day; each a 300-lb. projectile hurled with that fearful force. How can skulls and neckbones stand it? Yet they do; and the mighty brutes wheel off, ramping on their hind legs, like heraldic unicorns. Each strives to show the other fellow how fresh and unwinded he is. Then they back up, and go at it again— BANG!

Sometimes, though rarely, the horn may exercise another function—not of sledge hammer, but of sword. Baillie-Grohman records the taking of a ram "shortly after the rutting season, who had an immense cut, extending from the shoulder to the middle of his back; a wound undoubtedly inflicted by a rival."

But this is rarely the finish. Weight and endurance are what count. They wheel and charge and again, maybe half a dozen times before they prove the present problem, and show clearly, to the satisfaction of both, that 312 lbs. multiplied by 20 miles an hour and backed by 10 recuperative kilowatts is better than 340 lbs. multiplied by 20 miles an hour and backed by but 5 recuperatives. This is nature's try-out. For this they have trained; and for this, and by this, their race was made; for this they grew these mighty horns.

LIVES OF GAME ANIMALS, 1925–1927

White Sheep

In the great, glorious, rugged empire that extends un-spoiled from Kootenai to Kotzebue, we still find the Sheep in primitive habit. The evidence of countless hunters and of their photographs, is that the Sheep is a creature of the upland meadows; but retires for rest and security to the adjoining citadels of cliff and peak; as do seabirds that spend their lives roaming the restless sea, yet must, perforce, find on the rocky shore a place in which to rear their young.

As usual, the home range narrows on investigation. In the Yellowstone Park, the band that ranges over Mount Everts in the summer, merely descends in winter to the canyon of the Gardiner River, not 5 miles away, but 2,000 or 3,000 feet lower. Their whole lives may be spent within a 5-mile radius.

The uniformity of their lives and needs is modified chiefly by the weather. But they follow so much of routine that their little homeland is laid out in definite trails which they use with regularity, so that they have been deeply worn by generation after generation. . . .

The social order of the Thin-horned Sheep is like that of the Bighorned. I know of no differences.

Except during the rut, the big rams form a group by themselves, and are singularly harmonious, considering what awful rows they had not so long ago. When any trouble appears in this group, *"Cherchez la femme."*

The ewes and lambs, new and last year's, form another band that are under leadership of a wise old lady who is, most likely, the grandma of the lot. The 3-year-old rams in the big-boy stage, being not proper company for the ladies, and not quite fit to run with the men, form a third group, as a sort of hanger-on of the ewe-band.

As in the other Mountain Sheep, the present ruts in December, the craze lasting 6 weeks, from the last of November till the first week of January.

One ram appropriates all the ewes he can get, and seems good for as many as 40 or 50.

The young are born between mid-May and mid-June. They number usually one, but occasionally there are two or three.

They are weaned in August, but continue closely attached to the mother till the following May, when each has his nose put out of joint by his little baby brother now arriving. Still, he remembers that this is his mother; and, in some sense, follows her lead till his third year. Then he graduates into high school; that is, joins the semi-detached bachelor group that stands midway between the nursery and the club. This means the mother's ewe-band on one hand; and on the other, the care-free

The Dalglish Head
from Yukon

The Wilson Potter
Head. (dalli)

From Whitehorse probably
Length 35. girth 14½. tip to tip 19
Seems intermediate between
canadensis & dalli
Coll: McKay & Dippie, Calgary.

The white dall sheep, northernmost of North America's wild sheep, was seen by Seton on his several trips to Alaska and the Northwest Territories.

band of big, irresponsible father rams.

With these, they continue till, in their fourth or fifth year, they fight their way to a footing among the big fellows, and so establish their right to perpetuate the race.

LIVES OF GAME ANIMALS, 1925–1927

Bighorn

They were fairly matched, and frisked and raced alongside their mothers or fought together the livelong day. One would dash away, and the other behind him try to butt him; or if they came to an inviting hillock they began at once the world-old world-wide game of King of the Castle. One would mount and hold his friend at bay. Stamping and shaking his little round head, he would give the other to understand that *he* was King of the Castle; and then back would go their pretty pink ears, the round woolly heads would press together, and the innocent brown eyes roll as they tried to look terribly fierce and push and strive, till one, forced to his knees, would wheel and kick up his heels as though to say: "I didn't want your old castle, anyway," but would straightway give himself the lie by seeking out a hillock for himself, and, posing on its top with his fiercest look, would stamp and shake his head, after the way that, in their language, stands for the rhyming challenge in ours, and the combat scene would be repeated.

There could be only one end to such a wound: two hours, three hours at furthest, and then—well, never mind.

And the little one? He stood dumbly gazing at her. He did not understand. He only knew that he was cold and hungry now, and that his mother, to whom he had looked for everything . . . was so cold and still!

He did not understand it. He did not know what next. But we do—the lingering misery, and the inevitable finish, soon or late, according to his strength; and the Raven on the rock knew, and waited. Better for the Lamb, far better, quicker, and more merciful, had the rifle served him as it did his mother.

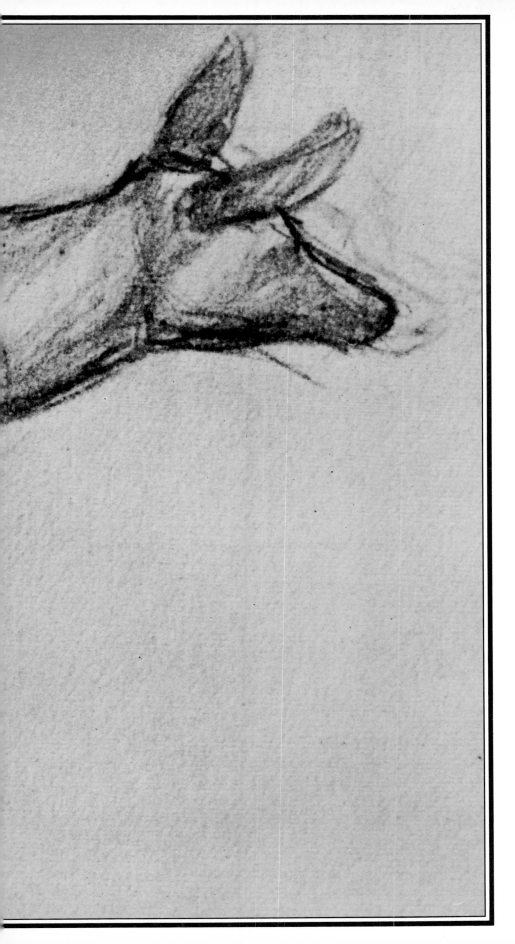

The Wolves were almost within leaping distance when Krag reached the shoulder-ledge. But a shoulder above means a ravine below. In a moment, at that call of distress, Krag wheeled on the narrow ledge and faced the foe. He stood to one side, and the three Ewes leaped past him and on to safety. Then on came the Wolves, with a howl of triumph. Many a Sheep had they pulled down, and now they knew they soon would feast. Without a pause they closed, but in such a narrow pass, it was one at a time. The leader sprang; but those death-dealing fangs closed only on a solid mass of horn, and back of that was a force that crushed his head against himself, and dashed him at his friend behind with such a fearful vim that both were hurled over the cliff to perish on the rocks. On came the rest. The Ram had no time to back up for a charge, but a sweep of that great head was enough. The points, forefronting now, as they did when he was a Lamb, speared and hurled the next Wolf, and the next; and then Krag found a chance to back up and gather his force. None but a mad Wolf could have failed to take warning; but on he came, and Krag, in savage glory of the fight, let loose that living thunderbolt—himself—and met the last of the furry monsters with a shock that crushed him flat against the rock, then picked him up on his horns as he might a rag, and **hurled** him farthest yet, and standing on the edge he watched **him** whirl and gasp till swallowed in the chasm.   LIVES OF THE HUNTED, 1901

Seton caught the stealth and timidity of this doe deer perfectly in this quick sketch.

Pronghorn

The ancient territory of the Pronghorns covered about 2,000,000 square miles; and a safe estimate, founded on the reports of travellers, would be 10 Antelope to every square mile. The present range covers about 1,000,000 square miles. But who will say that there are 10,000,000 wild Antelope left? If it be shown that there are 100,000 wild Antelope alive today I shall be agreeably surprised. At least half of them must be in Mexico.

These estimates are founded on many ancient and modern accounts, viewed in the light of my own experience.

During early days in New Mexico (about 1892) we could usually reckon on seeing a band of a dozen or 20 Antelope on the open plains every 10 miles or so during the fall. The region that I knew, and rode in daily, was some 60 miles long by 5 wide. In this were 5 well-known bands of Antelope, each keeping its own home locality and each numbering about 20. This would give 100 Antelope to 300 square miles. But all the "old-timers" agreed that there were _no Antelope_ in the country now. "Just an odd one here and there, and nothing to compare with the herds of the days gone by," they said.

In those early times bands of 2,000 or 3,000 were seen commonly on the plains of California.

Many years ago, while riding across the upland prairies of the Yellowstone, I noticed certain white specks in the far distance. They showed and disappeared several times, and began moving southward. Then, in another direction, I discovered other white flecks, which also seemed to flash and disappear. A glass showed them to be Antelope, but without wholly explaining the flashing or the moving, which ultimately united the two bands. I made a note of the fact, but did not understand it until the opportunity came to study Antelope in the Washington Zoo. I had been quietly watching the grazing herd on the hillside for some time; in fact, I was sketching, which affords an admirable opportunity for watching animals a long time minutely. I was so quiet that they seemed to have forgotten me, when, contrary to rules, a dog chanced into the Park. The wild Antelope has a habit of raising its head every few minutes while grazing, in order to keep a sharp lookout for danger, and these captives maintained the tradition of their race. The first that did so saw the dog. It uttered no sound, but gazed at the wolfish-looking intruder, and all the long white hairs of the rump-patch were raised with a jerk that made the patch flash in the sun. Each grazing Antelope saw the flash, repeated it instantly, and raised his head to gaze in the direction where the first was looking. At the same time I noticed on the wind a peculiar musky smell—a smell that certainly came from the Antelope—and was no doubt an additional warning.

Some time later I had opportunity to make a careful dissection of the Antelope's rump-patch, and the keystone to the arch of facts was supplied.

Coronado and his contemporaries, when they discovered the Antelope, were too busy adding to the spiritual Kingdom of their Masters, in consideration of the material plunder thereof, to bestow a second thought on this wonderful wild thing. It remained for Lewis and Clark, two hundred and seventy years later, to give the world detailed information about the Pronghorn of the Plains.

They comment with wonder on its great strength and its great weakness—that is, on its speed, which has given it first place for swiftness among the four-foots of America, and its inordinate curiosity, that has so often rendered its speed of no avail.

Greyhounds have doubtless caught many Antelope in open chase, but one greyhound cannot catch a full-grown, unwounded buck Antelope by fair running. As Governor St. John, of Kansas, said to Buffalo Jones after much experience, "It takes a mighty good greyhound to catch a mighty poor Antelope."

Once every day during the hours of sunheat the Antelope cautiously wend their way to some familiar pond, spring or

Unfinished oil of a young buck pronghorn.

stream. There they drink copiously, for they seem to need much water. Nevertheless, those who are familiar with the arid region of the continent will see at a glance that the map includes as Antelope range vast areas that are without water during the greater part of the year. How, then, do the Antelope live there? The answer is simple: These regions are provided with vegetation that has the power of storing up water for its own use—that can, during the few showers of winter, lay up enough moisture to carry it over the whole year; and chief among these provident plants are the great bulging cactuses. Each is a living tank charged with fluid so precious that it must perforce wear a bodyguard of poisonous bayonets to keep back the horde of wayfarers so ready to slake their thirst at the cactus's expense. In these the Antelope finds its desert springs. LIFE HISTORIES OF NORTHERN ANIMALS, 1909

Elk

I left camp about 8 A.M. There was six inches of snow on the ground, and it was still coming down—not a heavy fall, but just enough to veil the hills a quarter-mile off, and prevent me noting the landmarks.

I rode along a couple of miles north, then found the stale track of a big bull elk. I followed this for a mile or more . . . came on his bed, and near by the beds of two cow elk, all fresh; evidently they had heard me coming. I knew they would not go far till they had either seen me or smelled me. They could not smell me, for I had the wind. They must come back.

One way was open and downhill, the other uphill and brushy. I turned and rode downhill.

Sure enough, there was the big bull with horns and nose up high, seeking for me as I sought for him. It was too dark to photograph. I had no desire to shoot him, so I said: "Whoop!" He turned and steamed away; and so far as I know is going yet.

Then I got out pencil, paper, and foot rule, and sketched the three beds in the snow. This evidenced that the cows had been there all night. All was clear—the pellets and even the rubbings on an aspen trunk where the bull had scraped his horns. TRAIL OF AN ARTIST-NATURALIST, 1940

Sketches of whitetail catch the mood of feeding doe and alert buck. Drawings at far right show growth rate and shape of elk antlers from the first year as a "spike" bull through the eighth year when the horns began to degenerate into atypical conformation.

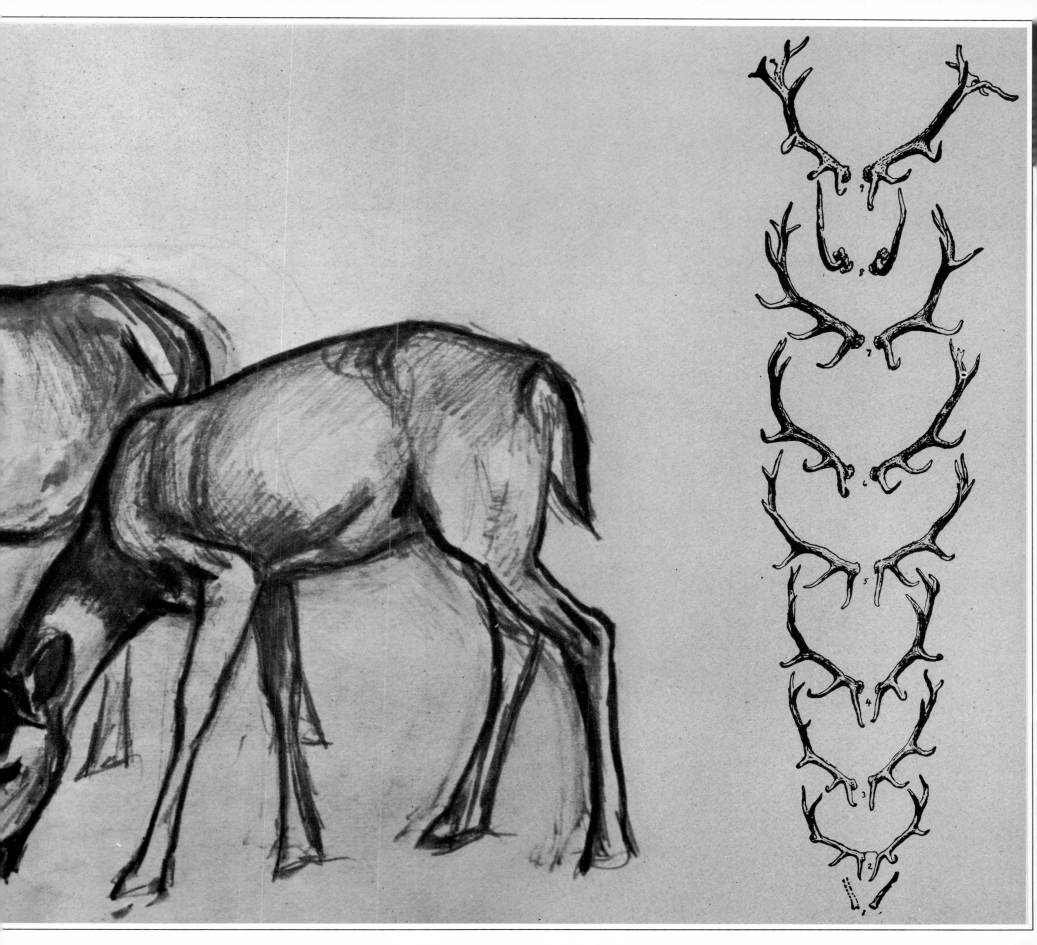

Cougar

From many hunting incidents that shed light or color on this freebooter's life, I select the following from my scrapbooks and journals: On the night of Sept. 14, 1899, I was camped with my wife on the High Sierra in California near Barker's Creek, not far from Mount Tallac. It does not rain there at that season, so we had no tent, but each night rolled up in our blankets and slept on the ground about half a yard apart. During that night there was a great alarm among the Horses. They broke loose and stampeded. Next morning we learned the cause. A Cougar had come into camp, had prowled around us as we slept, so said the tracks, but had gone off without attempting to harm any of us.

That is as near as I ever got to a wild Cougar. And although I have seen their tracks and their work many times in the Sierra, the Colorado Rockies, the Yellowstone, and the Bitterroots of Idaho, I never had the luck to see the living animal, though I doubt not many a one has watched me.

In mid-September, 1902, while camped in the Bitterroots of Idaho, I found in the dust the tracks of a band of Mule Blacktail moving all one way. I followed for a time and found the track of a large Cougar joining on. After a quarter of a mile, I came on the fresh-killed body of a female Deer and in the woods near by were her two fawns running about. But they were big enough to take care of themselves and made off.

Later, one of our party saw the Cougar but it calmly glided away keeping a tree trunk between itself and the rifleman.

On Jan. 27, 1914, I went on a Cougar hunt with Henry Anderson of Yellowstone Park. Our pack consisted of 2 trailing hounds and 2 Airedales—that is, 2 parts find and 2 parts fight. We rode over the slope of Mount Evarts past a dozen Bighorns, scores of Deer, hundreds of Antelope and thousands of Elk, but only one Cougar trail did we see: that was the big one we were after. At length we came on a large buck Blacktail just killed and partly devoured, but a driving snowstorm set in and ended all possibility of seeing, tracking, hearing, or shooting. . . . LIVES OF GAME ANIMALS, 1925–1927

Franklin's Ground Squirrel

This is the most active of the Ground-squirrels; even a terrier has little chance to catch it in its favorite undergrowth. It seems to know this very well, and will voice its shrill defiance again and again at the dog in pursuit.

I once put a Scrub Ground-squirrel into a cage with a Yellow Ground-squirrel that had been there for some time. At first it seemed afraid of its big cousin, but soon plucked up courage enough to attack and defeat him. It frequently uttered its loud musical whistle, while the Yellow one did nothing but chatter his teeth.

The next day I offered this individual some water. It drank greedily and noisily, but not copiously. Thus it differs from its two relatives in that it needs a supply of water. Perhaps this fact will be found important in its distribution.

The flesh-eating propensities of the group to which it belongs are well known, and the Gray Ground-squirrel offers no exception to the family habit. It is less carnivorous than the Striped species, yet loses no chance to eat a meal of flesh. The one from which I made the drawing gnawed its way out of the cage one night and ate the head off a newly mounted prairie-chicken before escaping for good.

LIFE HISTORIES OF NORTHERN ANIMALS, 1909

Chickaree

The seeds of spruce and fir seem to be the staples of this Squirrel's diet, but pine and maple are also largely drawn on. Its storage habits are precisely like those of its Eastern cousins, so far as recorded; for it makes innumerable caches, some of them large, under the duff banks that cover the ground beneath its favorite evergreens.

This burying of food is the unceasing, normal occupation of these Squirrels in the fall. In September, I found them hard at it in the Flattops of Colorado. Mearns's observations were made in early October. I doubt not from the time that the fir seeds have any pulp in them, till the frost comes, the Gray

In this magnificent head of a cougar, the artist evokes the singleminded concentration of the great cat, as if caught in a moment of stillness during a stalk.

Chickaree works at caching food. And much need he has for it, especially in the late winter and early spring.

My own observations on the species were made near Taos, N.M., and in Estes Park, Colo. I confess that I saw no trait in this Squirrel, and heard no sound from it, that seemed different from those of its red-headed cousin of the East.

If you go before the Arizona Legislature with a plea for this Chickaree, you are on a hopeless quest; at least, you are if you make an economic appeal. For the members say he is no use to agriculture, and the little good he does by planting trees, is offset by his destruction of cones and of birds' nests.

But go to the children of these men, and you have a better chance. In the Chickaree, they see embodied the joyous spirit of wild life in the woods; he is full of vivacity and tireless energy. They would not be without him in the summer camp for many tons of beef and flour. He is a fun-maker. They love him and appraise him far above material things outside their world.

Maybe in these things, the children are wiser than their elders. At any rate, they have influence; and, moreover, they have a majority. So Chickaree—the mischief-making Chickaree—is safe.

There is some evidence that this Squirrel migrates up and down the mountain, to avoid weather extremes; its summer haunts being near timberline, and its winter range lower down, even entering the pine zone for a way, so that its territory may temporarily overlap that of the big Tufted-eared Squirrel.

Its nests are constructed of pine needles, spruce twigs, and bark strips. They are placed on a convenient fork of some evergreen in the dense forest, and are usually 20 to 40 feet from the ground. One which I examined at Taos, N.M., was nearly 50 feet up in a pine, next the trunk. In structure, it was not distinguishable from the nest of the Eastern Red-squirrel.

Warren thinks that it also, to some extent, uses underground habitations.

Its voice and calls are much like those of the Eastern Red-squirrel. It has the same chatter and the same scolding tirade. Cary's remark that "its lively, cheering chatter is one of the few sounds which break the silence of the high mountain forests" is significant; and yet equally applicable to _douglasii_ and _hudsonicus;_ as well as to the present, and, indeed, to every form of Chickaree that I can get knowledge of.

LIVES OF GAME ANIMALS, 1925–1927

Bobcat

During a visit to northeastern Arkansas in the first week of Feb., 1920, I was told by several hunters that the high prices commanded by furs were stimulating the trappers to such an extent that Bobcats _(Lynx rufus)_ were getting scarce, and the immediate result of that was a marked and steady increase of wild turkeys.

The stalking of the turkeys, as well as the capture of Squirrels and Chipmunks, must have taken place in daylight, for the Wild-cat is a Lynx, and is lynx-eyed in full day.

But it is equally successful as a hunter in the dark. It is, in short, a Cat in its powers, needs, and ways of thinking.

Sometimes, by way of variant, it will, in sultry weather, follow the dry beds of streams or brooks to pick up the catfish, etc., or crayfish or frogs that remain in the deep holes of the creeks during the drought of summer.

So far, it has not been proven to dig out the eggs of turtles or to eat snakes or insects. Otherwise its bill of fare includes every living thing in the square mile that it considers home. Nor does it stop here if necessity drive. For the farm and the farmyard are really fine sources of revenue, provided an offset can be found for those unpleasant accessories, the Dogs and guns. The best answer to the problem is found in stealthy approach and black darkness. Like the Ocelot, it is a marvel in such raid work. Lambs, little Pigs, turkeys, geese, ducks, and chickens are acceptable in proportion to their size.

LIVES OF GAME ANIMALS, 1925–1927

The fluid, sinewy grace of the cat family is caught in these almost casual sketches of this feline, the cougar.

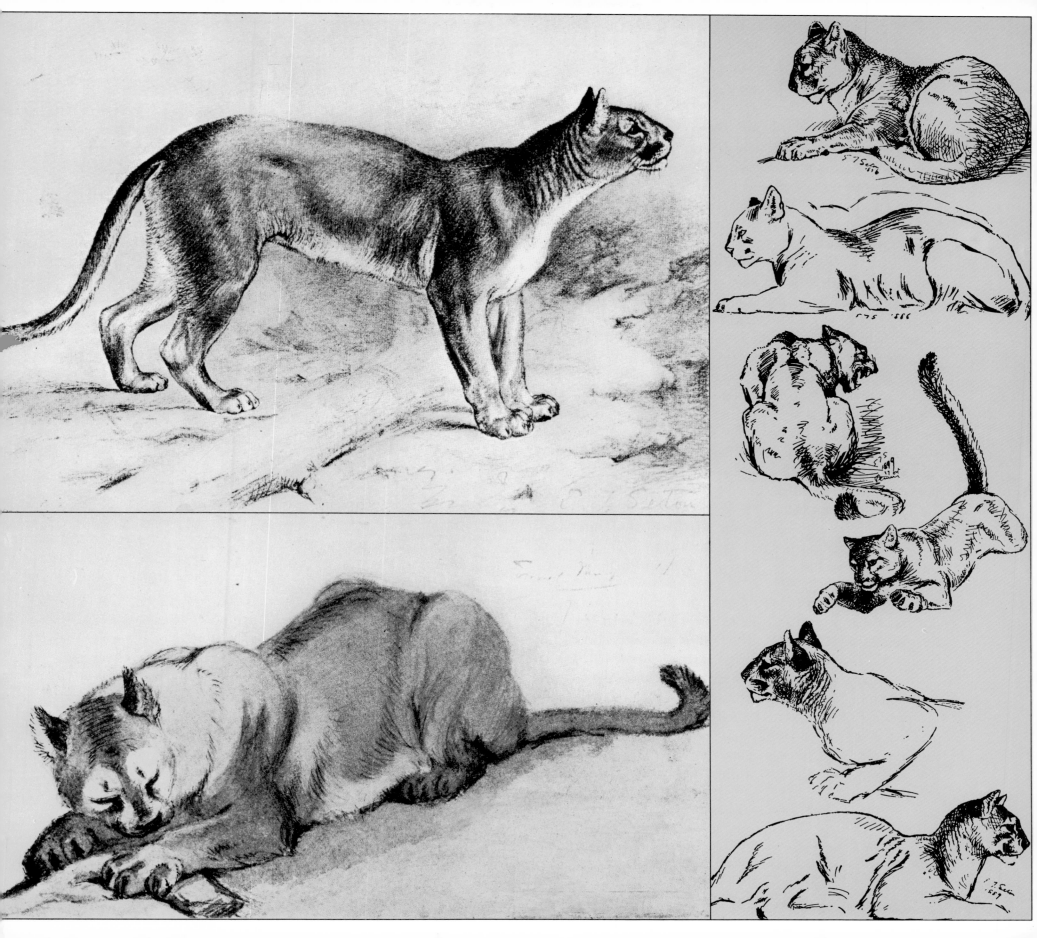

Prairie Hare

Who can adequately describe the wonderful thrill of delight—half animal, half poetic—that comes when first he sees a wild Deer bound away from his path? The old, old thrill, that dates from times when finding that Deer was a matter of life or death. This same vivific shock I never cease to get each time I see a White-tailed Jack-rabbit leap up from its nearby lurking place. It never fails to be two things—unexpected and superb. You never know where you may find a Jack—no one does—you never see it till it leaps at close range and lopes away on stiff four-cornered bounds, rising without effort, like an Antelope, and switching its great white brush from side to side like a miniature Whitetailed Deer; blazing with snowy white and punctuated with sharp black spots on his ears, it is the king of all its kind, the largest and finest of the Hares. The Black-tailed Jacks of New Mexico and California I got used to, without, however, entirely losing the little sudden taste of a naturalist's joy, as the live, lithe things sprung from my path; but the great Whitetail of the North, with its sudden leap into life and showy contrast on the plain, where a moment before it was a dead, invisible clod, never fails to give the hunter thrill that can scarcely be felt when we slowly creep up on a larger creature that we have watched and stalked for hours.

The Prairie-hare's pelt is so fragile, in fur and hide, that it does not constitute an acceptable barter stock, even where the fur-trade rivalry is keenest. The flesh is wholesome food, but has never achieved any popularity. It may yet establish itself as desirable game, to which high rank all sporting men should aim to help it as a measure of protection. But in making such apologetic enumeration of possible virtues, I feel myself guilty of something like special pleading, of making an appeal to the earthy jury, "called law-makers"; for after all, [the hare is] like so many I would save, without being able to prove their economic worth . . .

LIFE HISTORIES OF NORTHERN ANIMALS, 1909

Pika, the little haymaker of the rock slides near timberland in the western mountains, is an almost tailless relative of the hares and rabbits.

Jack Rabbit

A Jack-rabbit running from its enemy ordinarily covers eight or nine feet at a bound, and once in five or six bounds, it makes an observation hop, leaping not along, but high in the air, so as to get above all herbage and bushes and take in the situation. A silly young Jack will make an observation hop as often as one in four, and so waste a great deal of time. A clever Jack will make one hop in eight or nine, do for observation.

ANIMAL HEROES, 1905

Snowshoe Rabbit

While camped in the Bitterroot Mountains of Idaho, September 7, 1902, I saw something that looked like a social gathering among the Snowshoes. I had captured a half-grown one and at night put it under a box. It soon made the forest ring with a loud tattoo beaten on the box with its front feet. Shortly afterwards a full-grown Snowshoe-rabbit darted across the open camp space and into the dark forest again. Another and another appeared, and we heard the alarm thump in the woods around.

Armed with an acetylene lantern and a camera, my companion (W. E. Bemis) and myself went forth to investigate. As we set the lantern on the ground, a Rabbit rushed into the light, gazed at it and disappeared. Another came, gazed, gave an alarm thump and vanished. Then two came, then others, then more, a dozen Snowshoe-rabbits at length, were gazing into that marvelous light. One gave the alarm and all dashed off. But they came back, and yet closer, and began to caper about in the bright place and chase each other in play, leaping past the lantern which I held on the ground, and over the camera which my friend was holding.

At length one of them jumped on the camera between my friend's hands, and was caught. It shrieked with terror. In a twinkling every Rabbit had disappeared, and though we were two weeks longer in that second camp, we did not see another of this species.

LIFE HISTORIES OF NORTHERN ANIMALS, 1909

Rockchuck

The actual nest of the Rockchuck is in some snug cave or in the end of a crack that can be plugged and lined. One that I saw in the crags northwest of Cheyenne was 10 feet down a crevice that was a foot wide. It was of sticks, evidently carried up there by the owner. I could not get near enough to examine it. Another, the one I sketched, was in a cranny 15 feet up the cliff; it also was of sticks and roots, and beyond reach.

The few observations I could make, and the light of analogy, show that the castle is the abode of one family. As soon as the young are big enough, they leave home to seek some citadel for themselves.

High on some sunny crag that gives full fifty miles of view, the Rockchucks lie in the morning. There is nothing in their color or habits that suggests concealment. You can see the gleaming golden mantles half a mile away. But their eyes are as sharp as yours. Many sad experiences have taught their tribe that a man on foot is a man with a far-killer—a thing of thunder and death—and instantly the sprawling watchers are alert. A shrill, short whistle each sends forth, and every Marmot on this rock and every rock for half a mile, is keen agog, or rushes coverward to some safe hiding place.

Most of the summits are unscalable to man; but the Rockchuck has searched out every crevice, and usually has some secret climbway or narrow crack up which he can scramble to the very best and safest lookout.

For generations, these have been in use, as is proven by the vast accumulations of sign lodged in every cranny, and piled below the sloping sides. But the function of the watchers must have changed since the white man came—since the Buffalo,

Elk, Deer, and Antelope gave place to the "spotted Buffalo" of the range.

In those halcyon days, the redman with his bow took little count of the Whistler. Why should he, when the easier shot and bigger game brought ten times the hunter's spoils?

Yet the Rockchuck had his enemies. When he sallied forth to the rich feeding grounds about his castle, the Wolf, the Coyote, and the Bear were ready to nab him; and the eagle was at all times a menace, even when the Chuck was in seeming safety on his highest turret perch. For these it was that the watchman learned to use the welkin-reaching whistle—and thus resolved the riddle of his life.

There never yet was a big success without a train of feeble imitations—a great chief without a horde of satellites, glad to shelter behind his power. Many small creatures court the protection of the Whistler and his castle.

First among them, perhaps, is the two-barred Rockchip—the funniest, fattest little pot-bellied elfin that ever played brownie among the high constructed rocks of the Whistling Watchman's home. This comical Rock-squirrel settles down to eat the crumbs from the great one's table; and the keen-eyed watcher on the cliff announces without fail the eagle or the Fox, as well as the human hunters and all the other enemies of the Rock-squirrel—for are they not also his?

LIVES OF GAME ANIMALS, 1925–1927

Wolf

One night late in September after the last streak of light was gone from the west and the Coyotes had begun their yapping chorus, a deep, booming sound was heard. King took out his pipe, turned his head and said: "That's him—that's old Billy. He's been watching us all day from some high place, and now when the guns are useless he's here to have a little fun with us."

Two or three Dogs arose, with bristling manes, for they clearly recognized that this was no Coyote. They rushed out into the night, but did not go far; their brawling sounds were suddenly varied by loud yelps, and they came running back to the shelter of the fire. One was so badly cut in the shoulder that he was useless for the rest of the hunt. Another was hurt in the flank—it seemed the less serious wound, and yet next morning the hunters buried that second Dog.

Here in the narrowest place, where one wrong step meant death, the great Wolf turned and faced them. With forefeet braced, and head low and tail a little raised, his dusky mane abristling, his glittering tusks laid bare, but uttering no sound that we could hear, he faced the crew. His legs were weak with toil, but his neck, his jaws, and his heart were strong, and—now all you who love the Dogs had better close the book—on—up and down—fifteen to one they came, the swiftest first, and how it was done, the eye could scarcely see, but even as a stream of water pours on a rock to be splashed in broken jets aside, that stream of Dogs came pouring down the path, in single file perforce, and Duskymane received them as they came. A feeble spring, a counter-lunge, a gash, and "Fango's down," has lost his foothold and is gone. Dander and Coalie close and try to clinch; a rush, a heave, and they are fallen from that narrow path. Blue-spot then, backed by mighty Oscar and fearless Tige—but the Wolf is next the rock and the flash of combat clears to show him there alone, the big Dogs gone; the rest close in, the hindmost force the foremost on—down—to their death. Slash, chop and heave, from the swiftest to the biggest, to the last, down—down—he sent them whirling from the ledge to the gaping gulch below, where rocks and snags of trunks were sharp to do their work.

In fifty seconds it was done. The rock had splashed the stream aside—the Penroof pack was all wiped out; and Badlands Billy stood there, alone again on his mountain.

ANIMAL HEROES, 1905

Mule Deer

The antlers are very different from those of Whitetail, but resemble, somewhat, those of the Coast Deer. They are what scientists call dichotomous, that is, they are an arrangement of even forks, instead of having a main branch with snags. This, of course, is the type; the variations from it are endless, as suggested by the illustrations. Their history of growth is much the same as the Whitetail.

I stood gazing at the graceful creatures for a moment or two, then they moved off a little and commenced to rise in the air with a peculiar bounding movement, although without any apparent effort. They seemed to be playing, their movements were so entirely without any appearance of haste or alarm. It did not occur to me at first that they were running away. The idea I had in my mind of a Deer speeding was formed on seeing a dog or fox. I expected to see the laboured straining and the vast athletic bounds. But no! these evidently had not yet commenced to run, they seemed to be merely bounding up and down in the air, and it was only on noting the different hilltops which their feet touched lightly in succession and by seeing the fair, rounded forms rapidly becoming smaller in the distance that it dawned on me that *now* they were flying for safety.

Higher and higher they rose each time; gracefully their bodies swayed inward as they described a curve along some bold ridge, or for a long space the white bannerets seemed hanging in the air, while these wingless birds were really sailing over a deep gully. . . . When they were gone I went to their trail, where they had appeared to be rising and falling over the same place. Here was one track, where was the next? I looked all round, and was surprised to see a blank for 15 feet. I went on—another blank, and again and again. The blanks increased to 18 feet, then to 20 and then to 25. Each of these playful, effortless bounds covered a space of 18 to 25 feet. Ye gods! they do not run at all, they *fly,* and once in a while come down again to tap the hilltops with their dainty hoofs.

LIFE HISTORIES OF NORTHERN ANIMALS, 1909

Marmot

So far as I have seen, the burrows of the Whistler are exactly like those of the Yellow-footed Marmot—sometimes on an open hillside, by or under a flat rock or a great boulder, but invariably arranged so as to have the protection of massive rocks about the portal to the den. In regions where the Grizzly-bear abounds, the den is always among a heap of tumbled rocks, of a size and weight that have kept the creature's home life a secret from all naturalists; and, in most cases, offers an effectual obstacle to the entry of even a hungry Bear.

All the popular names of the Hoary Marmot connote its wonderful voice. Harmon, the old fur-trader, who first described the creature from the land side, said: "There is a small animal, found only on the Rocky Mountain, denominated by the natives *Quis-qui-su,* or *Whistler,* from the noise which they frequently make, and always when surprised, strongly resembling the noise made by a person in whistling."
The analogy of the Eastern Woodchuck would show that the species pairs, and that the mating takes place in the very early spring, as soon as the Marmots awaken from the winter sleep. But there are few observations on record to settle these many points.

In the Bitterroot Mountains of Idaho, in late Sept., 1902, I found a pair of Hoary Marmots associated on the same rock, and therefore, probably paired, as no others were about.

Marmots are good climbers. Why not, when their little brown brothers in the East climb trees? But these Marmots exercise their talents of this kind only in climbing some high, rocky pinnacle.

The Gray one loves a sunbath—all natural philosophers do; he loves the sense of security that comes from being on a high place—a common impulse in the wise. So he combines and gratifies these two strong instinctive cravings by climbing to some promontory inaccessible to Wolf or Bear . . .

LIVES OF GAME ANIMALS, 1925–1927

Begun and never completed, the painting portrays beautifully the alert quiescence of a young mule deer buck bedded down in the leaves.

The
perhaps
brown

M. Deer.

Some of them brown behind
less so on head — and all darker

Blacktail Deer

While in Denver, April 14, 1901, I was shown by Wm. R. McFadden a specimen of Coast Blacktail which he secured while hunting around Kootenai Lake in the Caribou Range, B.C., 60 miles N.W. of the Kootenai Lakes, about Oct. 28, 1892. He saw a band of 7 deer; 2 were bucks, 1 large and 1 smaller. He shot the large one, and was surprised to find it a *Coast Blacktail,* the only one he had ever heard of so far east. He followed the other for 5 miles in vain. The band was moving southwest.

This specimen I examined carefully, and sketched. It is in all respects a true Blacktail, except that it has the metatarsal gland 4 inches long; which raises a suspicion of hybridity. The tail is 7 inches long, without the hairs, which add 4 inches, and is of true *columbian* type.

As the Mule-deer is the creature of the half open, dry and hilly country, and the Whitetail the proper inhabitant of the brush-grown river bottoms, so the Blacktail is the Deer of the dense, damp forests of the western slope. It may be high at one season and low down at another; but in each case, its immediate normal surroundings is heavy unbroken timber. The rare occasions when it is found in upland prairies, merely show that it knows the value of a sunlight tonic; and like all wise foresters, submits its body periodically to the healing rays.

Another characteristic that the Blacktail shares with the Mule-deer is its peculiar bouncing action when in full flight. The Whitetail Deer leaps long and low. The Blacktail and the Mule-deer alone, of all swift things on legs, set off with all four feet close together as though "hogtied," rising very high and landing stiffly, to rise again in another wonderful high bound.

There is no doubt that the Whitetail fashion of running, like that of a Horse, is swifter and less tiring on a level course; but reference to the Mule-deer article shows the great advantage of the high bounding. It is for *climbing the hills* and overtopping the brush. So that among fallen rocks, in high

Like the practice of other artists, many of the author's sketches, such as the eyra cat at bottom, were made from photographs supplied him by other naturalists, hunters, explorers, and scientists.

chaparral or on steep hillsides, these Deer have nothing to fear in fair race from any quadruped native to their range. Indeed it guarantees to these two mountaineers a safety that would be impossible with any other gait.

A glimpse of its extraordinary swimming power is found in a record by Charles Sheldon during his trip to Admiralty Island, 1909: "In a heavy tide-rip 3 _miles_ off shore, two Deer, a buck and a doe, were seen swimming. They were headed across Frederick Sound for the mainland 9 miles distant. Evidently, a distance of 10 or more miles of intervening water is no obstacle for these Coast Deer."

My own experience with Blacktails is limited to a single hunting trip in the High Sierra about Lake Tahoe in the September and October of 1899. Deer were scarce; we saw only three or four, and got only one. But I lost no opportunity of making notes and sketches.

In some early accounts, the Blacktail is pictured as simple-minded, and an easy prey for the pot-hunter. But there is abundance of evidence to show that this innocent creature has fully responded to the urge of new conditions and modern guns, and now needs little help to maintain himself against any but the most skillful of hunters; provided always that his homeland be not hid in drifts of the ten times accursed snow.

LIVES OF GAME ANIMALS, 1925–1927

Eyra Cat

This elegant Weasel-cat is at home in the dense, thorny thickets of the lower Rio Grande. Mesquite, cat-claws, granjeno, chaparral, acacia, ironwood, cactus—oh, how they all run thorny in that country!—are fearsome as barb-wire to man and the bigger beasts, but to the little Eyra they are the armed and friendly sentinels of his castle doorway, or the wire entanglements of his safest entrenchment.

Partly due to the fact that its home garden is impenetrable to man or Dog, and partly due to its elusive, furtive, and almost strictly nocturnal habits, the slim Eyra is supposed to be extremely rare.

LIVES OF GAME ANIMALS, 1925–1927

Armadillo

The Armadillo is everywhere covered with beautiful, sculptured and regular horny plates, even on the ears where they are very small and delicate. On the inner side of the legs and on the belly, where not needed, rigid economy has reduced the plates to little or nothing, using instead the cheaper material of bristles, a few of which are scattered on the back between the bony plates and bands. The body armour is broken by 9 rings or banded joints, which are broad on the sides, and narrow on the back, where, indeed, they are reduced to 8.

The tail has 14 rings—horny joints that look as though they would telescope into each other—and a final 4 or 5 inches of scaly tip, like the tail of a snake sticking out of the last joint.

The sharp, strong claws or hooflets, when well worn, remind one of the claws of a turkey that has had to scratch gravel all summer.

The long, thin, extensile tongue is covered with a stuff as sticky as fly-paper. This the creature shoots out, and lashes about among insect swarms; and so feeds riotously on what most animals would consider not proper food.

So much for the dry details of this little armoured car. But one must have had a long training in medieval harness-equipment to appreciate the exquisite hand-made workmanship on this extraordinary little brute. Its armour is of harmonious make throughout, of the hardest available material; yet no two portions of it are quite the same. Each part has a style suited to its own brunt or need of souplesse. The whole is a combination of case armour, chain mail, and metal bosses on leather—Roman, Saracen, and Middle English, whichever best suits the need—and softly graded into each other. It looks as though hand-made by a smith of consummate skill, an armourer and an artist. LIVES OF GAME ANIMALS, 1925–1927

Wolf Hunt

During that summer of 1893 I was several times in New York; and while there always ran out to Plainfield, New Jersey, to see the Fitz-Randolph family. Our conversation ever turned to his cattle ranch in New Mexico, and the terrible toll taken yearly by the wolves. Fitz-Randolph said the cattle business would yield big dividends if we could curb those wolves, but they defied all the best efforts of cowboys, gunmen and trappers.

Oh, how I did long to go on a campaign against those wolves! I knew I could meet them and beat them, but I dared not take the time. My duties held me bound. I was working all day at the easel, and every night till late at my desk.

The task was agreeable enough, and it all went in the direction of my ambition. But I was under a terrible handicap. Minute work, desk work, twelve and fifteen hours a day, was too much. Terrible excruciating pains were centered in my eyes. I tried different glasses. Finally, my doctor said: "Now, my friend, unless you wish to go totally blind, you will quit all desk and easel work and go for a long holiday in the wilds."

Then clear focus was given the thought by an offer from Fitz-Randolph. He said: "If you will go to my ranch in New Mexico, and show the boys some way of combating the big cattle-killing wolves, I will pay all expenses, and let you make whatever you can out of bounties and hides. But you must promise to spend at least a month on the ground at the work." . . .

I reached Clayton, New Mexico, at 11 P.M., October 22, 1893; and put up at the Clayton House. . . .

On Tuesday, October 24, I got a thirty-mile lift with the mail carrier, Hubert Crouse, to Clapham post office, the nearest point to the Fitz-Randolph ranch, known locally as the L Cross F outfit.

Here I learned that, owing to the absence of the foreman, H. M. Foster, and the resignation of the cook, I was not to go to the head ranch on Penabetos Creek; but, by arrangement, board with one Jim Bender, a bachelor whose small holding was on the Leone Creek four miles northwest of Clapham.

Bender was on hand with a buckboard for my baggage, and thenceforth he and I lived together in his lonely little ranch house.

Coyotes were plentiful. We saw two or three every day, and heard many at night. Jackrabbits and prairie-dogs abounded, but not a sign of a gray wolf did I see.

"No," said Jim, "we never see them in the daylight. If we did, we could kill them with a long-range rifle. But I'll show you lots of their work."

This he did, mostly the carcasses of yearling calves, with the hindquarters partly eaten, the rest left for coyotes.

Back of the ranch house, a quarter-mile, was a precipitous rocky hill known as Mount Tabor, named after a previous owner of the ranch. This was 200 feet high. One day I climbed it, and, in accordance with an old custom of the West, had built a stone obelisk to mark the highest point. Suddenly I noticed on the plain below me two coyotes, probably male and female, for they commonly hunt in pairs. I kept out of sight, and watched them.

One coyote crouched behind a thick greasebush, the other walked openly toward a prairie-dog that was yapping on its mound. He made a half-hearted rush as the prairie-dog dived. The coyote far back behind the greasebush now rushed forward, and crouched beside a bush that was only six feet from the prairie-dog hole. Meanwhile Coyote No. 1 sauntered slowly forward. Presently the prairie-dog peeped out. He saw that Coyote No. 1 was at a safe distance, and that he was going still farther away. The yapper became bold; he stepped right out and yapped at Coyote No. 1. Coyote No. 2 rushed forward, and almost got him. In this case the trick failed, but obviously it must often be successful.

I lost no time in beginning my wolf hunt. The wolves had killed seven colts and five sheep close to this settlement within the past three days. In the region was a wolf-hunter named Joe Callis who had killed 109 gray wolves in six weeks. He had used strychnine only. This was the latest available information.

This particular wolf (derived from the large painting on page 88) was admired by Theodore Roosevelt. Seton made a separate painting of it and gave it to the then-president . . . a personal friend and fellow naturalist.

I had come prepared for a poison campaign.

Numerous experiments showed me many things. The wolves were my teachers.

Eventually this was the plan I adopted: When killing a beef for ranch use, take the pluck, *i.e.,* the heart and lungs together, for a drag; make a bag of the fresh rawhide, touch it not at all with the bare hands, and as little as possible with the steel knife. Wear leather gloves rubbed with fresh blood. Do not breathe on it. Enclose two grains of strychnine in a gelatine capsule, cut baits of beef or suet, two by three inches, make a hole in each with a sharp bone, push in the capsule. A pair of wooden pinchers is necessary to lift the baits. Finally, make a drag by fastening the pluck of the beef to your rope which is looped on your saddle horn. This trails on the ground twenty feet behind your horse; and at every quarter-mile or less, you lift a poison bait from the bag and drop it on the trail.

The theory is that a wolf or coyote will strike this trail, and follow it eagerly. Coming to the bait, he will gobble that and still follow; so that he dies on the line and is easily found. But for that, he might go a quarter-mile to one side and die in a thicket, never to be discovered.

With coyotes this worked perfectly well. Many and many a coyote did I get, by means of poison, but never once a gray wolf.

Then two incidents happened which gave me plenty of food for thought.

Early one morning I was riding the drag of the day before, when I saw, nearly a quarter-mile ahead, a coyote also on my drag. He stopped at something, evidently a poison bait, and devoured it. He went on 200 yards, then fell in the first horrible convulsion of strychnine poisoning. I galloped up, and drew my gun to end his suffering. The ball went over his head. However, now he knew his enemy. He staggered to his feet, vomited all he had in his stomach, then sought to escape. He dragged his paralyzed hind legs on the ground, but worked desperately with the fore-feet, snapping at his own flank and legs with frenzied jaws.

I rode and fired again—and again missed. He made another desperate effort.

I followed fast and far, and soon realized that I was making him take the remedy that was the only successful solution: "puke up the poison, get up and fight for your life."

I fired again and again, but gradually his desperate efforts found response in his hind legs. He drove his will power into them—they worked—he went faster and faster; and, at length, although I followed for half a mile on a good horse, he gradually faded away and was finally lost in a great stretch of scrubby gullies.

These things I now realized: Had I let him alone, he would have died where first he took the bait; but I made him take the one possible remedy—get up and fight for his life. Next, he would ever after know and fear the smell of strychnine, and would teach other coyotes to do the same.

I had often found my poison victims with gashes on loins and on limbs; I know now that these were self-inflicted in their agony.

The Winchester repeating rifle had long been the favorite on the cattle ranges. But a rival firm came out this year with a tremendously advertised rifle that was guaranteed to put the Winchester out of business.

My dear Aunt Schreiber heard about this from her men friends in Toronto, and determined that I should have one for Christmas. To make quite sure of its arrival on time, she expressed it to me more than a month in advance. Thus it was that I was equipped with the new Blanketty gun early in November; and, after a few trial shots, put it in my saddle scabard in the place that usually held my Winchester.

In consequence of this infidelity to the tried and proven, I one day (November 17, 1893) had a curious accident, that by all rules, should have ended my career. In a certain promising area, where tracks of gray wolves as well as coyotes abounded, I needed a large bait; so I selected a big-jawed steer of unusual size—a three- or four-year-old. As long as I drove him with the bunch, he was all right —just a little wild. But when I cut him out, it was hard work. He kept dodging back, defying me, and got snuffy, as they say there; that is, letting off little angry snorts, shaking his horns, and raising his tail very high. Still I maneuvered him to the point where I meant to kill him.

By this time my horse, as well as the steer, was all excitement. I could not shoot with certainty from the saddle, so I did as often before—I leaped to the ground, and threw the reins over the horse's head, knowing that every well-trained cow-pony will stand still at the very spot where the reins touch the ground. My pony was well trained; but when I threw the reins over his head, I did not look to see if they touched the ground; my eyes were all on the angry steer before me.

Apparently the reins caught on his right ear, and hung high. The horse was free; and at once trotted off, without my knowledge.

I kneeled for steadiness and levelled my new rifle at the steer as he raced toward me.

Click—and the gun missed fire. Again I pulled, and again a *click*. Three times I tried to jerk in another cartridge. The breech was jammed.

The steer was now within twenty feet of me, coming on. I turned quickly to jump on my horse. *The horse was a hundred yards away, trotting ever farther.* I saw my finish—I knew nothing could save me from that enraged steer, but one thing. I did that.

I froze into a graven image. I neither rose nor blinked, but sat kneeling, and still. The steer leaped over me, and dashed away to join the distant herd.

I do not mention the name of that rifle here and now. Apparently its breech action always jammed in cold weather, when the lubrication was stiffened into wax. My friends and I have stuck to the good old Winchester ever since.

TRAIL OF AN ARTIST-NATURALIST, 1940

Ocelot

His favorite surroundings are impenetrable thickets so dense that Dogs can hardly get in and hunters not at all. In a square mile of chaparral, a dozen Ocelots might pass their whole lives unknown to any man; for they need never venture out and hunters cannot venture in. Their every forthgoing is nocturnal, so that they easily escape all notice of their arch-enemy. Indeed, the Ocelot has the reputation of being able to conceal himself more effectively than any other large animal in America.

To complete his furtive modes of life, he loves the darkness so whole-heartedly that moonlight, and even starlight, seem to put a check on his enterprise and daring. Having passed the day behind the safe barb-wire entanglements of his chaparral home, he waits till the evening light is gone and the dusk has given place to dark. A black and stormy night is much to his taste. On such a night, he will boldly risk the Dogs that guard the barnyard, and make poultry raids that he would never dream of in calm weather or moonlight. How he finds his various prey aloft in such a time of noise, wind, and blackness, is a puzzle and a tribute indeed to the accuracy of the creature's senses. Yet he does find them, and according to all authorities, climbs the trees, going direct to roosting fowls, carrying off half-a-dozen in a night, and leaving sometimes a number killed that he could not carry off—just as some other burglars, when alarmed by danger of discovery, may hurry off, leaving a part of their swag behind them.

The Ocelot is a forest-loving animal, and is just as much a tree-climber as our common Cat, which means that he is not in the Squirrel and Monkey class, but he can climb easily and quickly whenever his purpose is served by so doing. He often goes bird-nesting up aloft; he even takes a noonday nap upstairs, and commonly betakes himself to a tree when in danger from his racial enemies of the Dog tribe. Ordinarily, however, his life is spent on lower levels. He frequents dense cover—either heavy timber, thorny thickets, or rocky hillsides . . .

LIVES OF GAME ANIMALS, 1925–1927

Kangaroo Rat

And now he is once more skimming merrily over the mud and sands of the upland plains; shooting across the open like a living, feathered arrow; tempting the rash Coyote to thrust his unfortunate nose into those awful cactus brakes, or teaching the Prairie Owls that if they do not let him alone they will surely come to grief on a Spanish bayonet; coming out by night again to scribble his lacework designs on the smooth places, to write verses of measured rhythm, or to sing and play hop-scotch in the moonlight with his merry crew.

Soft as a shadow, swift as an arrow, dainty as thistle-down, bright-eyed and beautiful, with a secret way to an underground world where he finds safety from his foes—my first impression was not so very far astray. I had surely found the Little Folk, and nearer, better, and more human Little Folk than any in the nursery books. My chosen flinty track had led me on to Upper Arcadie at last. And now, when I hear certain purblind folk talk of Fairies and Brownies as a race peculiar to the romantic parts of England, Ireland, or India, I think:

"*You* have been wasting your time reading books. You have never been on the shifting Currumpaw when the moon of the Mesas comes up to glint the river at its every bend, and bathe the hills in green and veil the shades in blue. You have not heard the moonlight music. You have not seen these moonbeams skip from thistle-top and bayonet-spear to rest in peace at last, as by appointment, on the smooth-swept dancing-floor of a tiny race that visits this earth each night, coming from nowhere, and disappearing without a sound of falling feet.

"You have never seen this, for you have not found the key to the secret chamber; and if you did, you still might doubt, for the dainty moonlight revellers have coats of darkness and become invisible at will.

"Indeed, I believe you would say the whole thing was a dream. But what about the lace traceries in the dust? They are there when the sun comes up . . ." LIVES OF THE HUNTED, 1901

The muskrat—caught at its usual wet chores—was with Seton throughout his life. Note its "push-up" or house in the right background.

White Goat

The first time I met the White Goat, was in Glacier Park; and the impression it gave me, was of snow lodged in a cave or on a shelf of the far, sheer precipice. Very soon I saw more flecks, and noted that these flecks of snow were all nearly of one size and shape, and were faintly tinged with yellow; then it dawned on me that these were Mountain Goats. It was hard to believe that anything on four legs could get to such places, much less elect to stay there.

As I came nearer, the Goats suggested common fleecy Sheep, new-washed for the shearing. And when close enough to make them go off at their slow, ambling pace, I thought at once of a White Bear, and remembered that Captain Cook probably saw the skin, and passed it for that of a little Bear.

When Mother Nature decided to create an animal that could and would be happy in the uninhabited steeples that crown the great cathedral of the Rockies, she selected as raw material some hoofed thing of the lower levels, blessed him with a dauntless heart, nerves of iron, limbs of steel, and a coat of warmest wool, plentifully reinforced in an abundance of long, coarse guard hairs. Then she bleached her new plaything till he was pure white, and bade him go forth in the promised land, where none were disposed to envy him or question his exclusive right.

It is proof of dry, unbroken cold in his native realm that the robe, so completely resistant to wind and frost, is a poor protection against rain. In the N.Y. Zoological Park, the Goat herd has been managed with great success by Keeper Bernard McEnroe. He early learned that the creatures cannot stand rain. He shuts up the herd under cover as soon as a rainstorm begins. If they were exposed to a drenching storm for 24 hours, their coats would water-log, and the chances are that pneumonia would carry off the lot.

In their native wilds, it will be seen later, the Goats have caves of refuge for bad weather.

The fleecy underwear, that has won for him the name of "the only American Woolbearer," is 3 to 4 inches long, snowy white, and fine as merino.

G. B. Grinnell says: "Specimens which I furnished some years ago to Dr. Thomas Taylor, microscopist of the Agricultural Department at Washington, were called by some wool experts fine Cashmere wool; by others, Australian fine; and by still others, fine wool from various foreign ports. Doctor Taylor pronounced the wool finer than Cashmere wool."

Long ago, the natives of the Goat country learned to spin this wool, and weave it into blankets. They gathered the wool either from the bushes or from the dead Goat; and spun it on the bare thigh, with the flat left hand, while the right hand held a spindle that gathered up the thread. Then with a warp of twisted cedar bark, strung on the simplest kind of a loom, and balls of this wool dyed yellow, brown, and black with native dyes, they wove the famous Chilkat blankets—each one a symbolic record of some totemic animal—a futurist, cubist, impressionistic design, so artistic and full of worth that Chilkat blankets vie with those of the Navaho, as the most beautiful the world has seen.

The Goat is an exception to nearly every known rule; and he is an amazing and gratifying exception to the rule that man has wiped out nearly all the big game of America. For the land that the Goat inhabited 400 years ago, it still inhabits; and so far as we can learn, its numbers are the same.

If, then, we make a careful estimate of the present number of Goats, we shall probably know the ancient population.

When I was in the Glacier National Park in 1916, I used every means to get an estimate of the Goats that frequent the higher half of its 2,500 square miles. Most of the guides agreed that there were about 3,000. But Tom Dawson, with longer experience than the others, was sure that that estimate was too low; 4,000 he thought was nearer the truth. Let us call it 3,500; which gives a rate of 3 to the square mile.

If, on some lowering morning when clouds and flying scud are

Coyotes were a part of Seton's youth on the Manitoba prairies and, at the time of his death, all around him in his beloved New Mexico.

drifting low over Manhattan, one could look from the Times Building, out and up to those higher peaks, the Equitable, the Metropolitan, and the Woolworth, and see white creatures—Goats, incredible Goats—crawling along the cornices, pulling themselves up on the turrets, or calmly chewing their cud as they lay looking down from the weather vanes, we should have much the same sensation as in watching the bearded mountaineer in this cloud-hung, perpendicular home.

What a perfect model he is for all mountaineers! He never lopes, and rarely trots; he is never in a hurry; and never moves till he is sure. No matter how great his danger, he plays the safe game, and makes slow haste to get out of sight. Not even when a month-old kid, can he be rattled by peril. Never once has hunter made him hurry his calm march, never in history has he been stampeded. In thunder, earthquake, or landslide, it is the same. You cannot shake his nerve by shooting. The shots may be falling all around him, but he never turns his bearded head or jumps; he seems neither to see nor hear you; but fixes all his attention on the trail he is picking out, and climbs fearlessly where no other four-foot on earth could follow.

He does not hesitate to jump down 20 or 25 feet to a lower ledge; and no matter how icy it be, his hoofs are sure to grip. No one ever saw him miss his footing; with him there is no such thing as slipping or falling. He cannot leap upward very

far, seldom attempting more than 3 or 4 feet. But I have heard the hunters describe his way of rearing on his hinder legs to reach up 5 or 6 feet, and hook his front hoofs over a higher narrow ridge; then, like a trapeze performer, haul himself up to some other impossible-looking shelf overhanging the abyss. Similarly, if there be head room, he can turn on a 6-inch ledge by rearing upright on his hinder legs; then facing about to drop on to all four feet, headed the other way.

LIVES OF GAME ANIMALS, 1925–1927

Chink

He was a mere Puppy yet, and a little fool in many ways, but away back of all was a fibre of strength that would grow with his years. The moment that Coyote tried to follow into the tent—his master's tent—Chink forgot all his own fears, and turned on the enemy like a little demon.

The beasts feel the force of right and wrong. They know moral courage and cowardice. The moral force was all with the little scared Dog, and both animals seemed to know it. The Coyote backed off, growling savagely, and vowing, in Coyote fashion, to tear that Dog to ribbons very soon. All the same, he did not venture to enter that tent, as he clearly had intended doing.

Then began a literal siege; for the Coyote came back every little while, and walked round the tent, scratching contemptuously with his hind feet, or marching up to the open door, to be met at once, face to face, by poor little Chink, who, really half dead with fear, was brave again as soon as he saw any attempt to injure the things in his charge.

One night, when she got a response, she yielded to the impulse again to call, and soon afterward a large dark Coyote appeared. The fact that he was there at all was a guarantee of unusual gifts, for the war against his race was waged relentlessly by the cattlemen. He approached with caution. Tito's mane bristled with mixed feelings at the sight of one of her own kind. She crouched flat on the ground and waited. The newcomer came

stiffly forward, nosing the wind; then up the wind nearly to her. Then he walked around so that she should wind him, and raising his tail, gently waved it. The first acts meant armed neutrality, but the last was a distinctly friendly signal. Then he approached, and she rose up suddenly and stood as high as she could to be smelled. Then she wagged the stump of her tail, and they considered themselves acquainted.

LIVES OF THE HUNTED, 1901

Coyote

The voice of the Coyote is one of its most remarkable gifts. Barking is supposed to be limited to the Dog and the Coyote. This is not strictly true, for Wolves, Foxes, and Jackals bark at times, but it is true that the Coyote is the only wild animal of the family that habitually barks.

We must assume, as general propositions, that nothing in nature is without adequate cause, and that it is always worth while to search that out. Most of the many calls of the Coyote are signals to its companions, but some of them seem to be the outcome of the pleasure it finds in its own music.

The most peculiar of its noises is the evening song, uttered soon after sunset, close to camp at times. This is a series of short barks, increasing in power and pitch till it changes into a long squall. One Coyote begins, and immediately two or more join in, making so much noise that newcomers think there must be a hundred Wolves out there. It is kept up for perhaps a minute or two, then ceases till some new impulse seizes them. Aug. 27, 1904, in W. F. White's menagerie at Winnipeg, I saw a Coyote pup, which, though little bigger than a House-cat and less than 3 months old, had a fully developed voice, and, much to the amusement of numerous bystanders, joined in the yapping chorus as lustily as his grown-up relatives. I think that both sexes sing.

I never heard the chorus among wild Coyotes while the sun was above the horizon. In the evening, it comes first with the gloaming, and in the morning is unknown after dawn.

LIVES OF GAME ANIMALS, 1925–1927

These young deer, one with ears cocked, reveal why Odocoileus hemionus *is called the mule deer.*

Cauodeau Bridge
drawn in Kansy Pikurs Zoo
Zorouto 1845
by Pauel de Cato

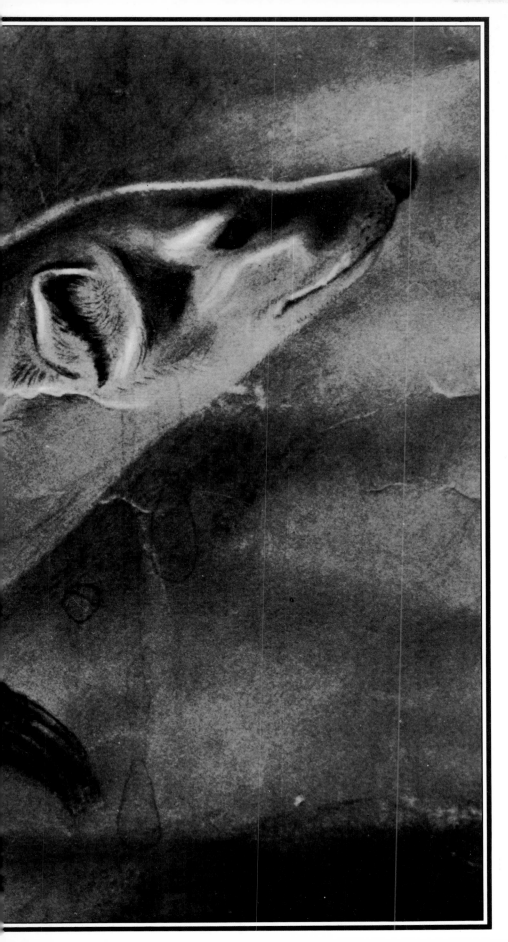

Badger

The Badger is a winter-sleeper. A "seven-sleeper," the country folk say. It generally appears above ground as soon as the snow is gone. In the early days of Manitoba, before the fence and the plough had come, the traveller saw, hourly, on the sunny mornings, a whitish bump on a raised mound of earth not far from the trail. As he approached it, the white bump might develop a sharp and movable point at one end, the point would sway in the wind, then the white thing disappear into the earth, showing that the bump was simply a Badger taking his morning sun-bath. On the Souris Plains Badgers were thus seen a dozen times a day.

They rarely go far from their holes, and when they do, they are much alarmed by discovery, and go shuffling about to each promising place in search of a road to the friendly shelter of mother earth.

I overtook one once on the open plains in Arizona. He skurried about but could find no hole, so faced about, and as he made short leaps towards my companion I caught him by the only safe handle, his rough, strong tail. But possession seemed to satisfy the hunter's instinct, and once we had conquered him we freed him and left him in peace.

On another occasion, in June, 1897, on the Upper Yellowstone, I met a Badger waddling over the prairie. I had a camera with me and, meaning to get a picture, ran after him. To my great surprise, he came rushing towards me uttering a loud snarling. Fully believing in my ability to avoid his attack, if indeed he really meant to make one, I continued to run, when, just as we were within thirty feet of each other, he fell tail-first into a shallow badger-hole that he had not seen, and I fell head-first into another I had not seen. We both were greatly surprised, quite shocked indeed, but he recovered first. He scrambled out of his pitfall, ran ten feet nearer to me, then dived down his home-hole, towards which he had been making from the first. LIFE HISTORIES OF NORTHERN ANIMALS, 1909

No wonder the badger lived as a digging animal—notice the length and size of the claws. See page 134 for other informal sketches of this Great Plains member of the weasel family.

Packrat

The outstanding, visible, and omnipresent evidence of the Packrat's presence is the nest. This is a vast and growing pile of sticks, stones, leaves, pine cones, cactus, thorns, bones, cow-dung, bark, rubbish, and trash galore. The Rat weighs half a pound; the mound weighs half a ton.

The cactus or other spines are a dominating feature of the mound. They fringe and protect it everywhere, and are especially thick and dangerous around the doorways, as we know to our cost whenever trying to force an entrance.

In the center of this mound is the real nest—a long chamber about 5 inches across and 3 high. It is lined, roofed, and floored with a mass of the finest available shreddings—usually chewed cedar bark—but also some hay, hair, feathers, and fur, with cotton and rags when available.

The outer walls may be rugged and spiney, but this innermost sanctuary is always a model of cosiness and soft comfort.

There are several entrances, most of them visible and aboveground; but the prudent mound-builder always has a cyclone cellar into which he can retreat in times of unusual stress.

The nest of the Packrat, like the dam of the Beaver, is never finished. As long as he lives there, the sedulous little one keeps piling on new material; and he will live there as long as fate lets him. Not a night passes without additional sticks and rubbish being added; so that, as the years go by, the nest becomes a little mountain composed of a ton or more of trash.

There is one menace to the nest and to the Rats, that has always loomed large, and as far back as history goes—whether before that, is uncertain. That menace is wild-fire. In seasons of drought, the fires which sweep the forest and mesas of the Southwest, find a ready-made pile of kindlings in the dry, upstanding nest of the Packrat. In a few minutes, the mound is

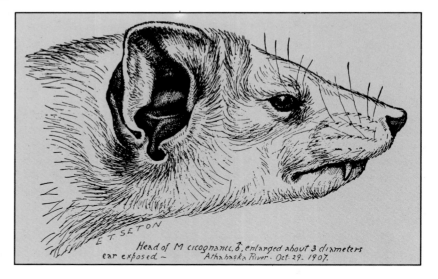

Head of M cicognanii, ♂, enlarged about 3 diameters
ear exposed ~   Athabaska River - Oct. 29. 1907.

converted into a glowing pile of coals, with smoke and scorching breath ascending.

The most amazing propensity of the Packrat is the one from which he gets his name—the mania for gathering in one place a collection of bright, curious, unusual, or interesting (but quite uneatable) things—a museum of his own. It is akin to his food-storage and to his nest-building impulses. Yet it has developed into something quite different from either.

There is scarcely any object, unusual and small enough, that the Packrat will not add to his museum, especially if it glitter, or, in some way, catch the eye. I have seen nesting mounds made of cactus spines and cow-dung; but the museum exhibit on the top comprised shells, pebbles, pine cones, twigs, sticks, cactus prickles, seed pods, bits of tin and china, old cartridges, broken buckles, rags, leather scraps, feathers, skulls of small animals. I have heard of every movable kind of personal property in the collection, including a bottle of oil, a pair of spectacles, a set of false teeth, a box of matches, and a stick of dynamite.

The second baffling instinct—the one for which he gets his name of "Trade-rat"—is even harder to explain than the foregoing—that is, his habit of exchange. When he pilfers some useless bauble from the ranchman's house, he commonly leaves in its place a product of his own domain. For example, he may carry off the silver spoons, and fill the empty place with toadstools; lug off the kitchen clock, and on its shelf set up a Rabbit's skull; empty the box of chocolates, and fill it up again with cow-chips.   LIVES OF GAME ANIMALS, 1925–1927

Prairie Dog

Haunts of the Black-tailed group are level, open, dry, clay country, either wide plains or flat valley lands. This Barker, as much as the Antelope, is a creature of the wide open spaces.

On the other hand, the White-tailed Prairie-dog's special domain is the Rocky Mountain region of the United States. They show a liking for rough surroundings—canyons, mesas, ridges, scrubby and rocky places, rarely below the 6,000-foot level.

So far as I could see or learn, a Prairie-dog never goes a hundred yards from home. His life is spent on his own front yard, a skimp half-acre.

This exception, however, must be recorded. Once in a while, for reasons not set forth by anyone or understood, and yet most obviously satisfactory, the whole population of a dog-town has been known to get up some fine day, forsake home, household effects, land and native ridge, then emigrate to parts unknown, some miles away. All of us who rode the Plains in the old days of the West, can recall the abandoned dog-towns that frequently were met with. Sometimes it seemed that the petering out of the food supply imposed this going. But on some occasions, this was evidently not the case; and guessing at the cause, we talked of rattlesnakes, Blackfooted Ferrets, changing water tables, and disease; yet without reaching any conclusion.

Like every creature on this list that has been able to hold its own against man, the Yap-rat's safety is in Mother Earth.

When first one sees a dog-town on the plain, the obvious and distinctive feature is the earth mound at the door of each den. Usually this is about a foot high, and 3 or 4 feet in diameter; but the "mound increases in size with age, those that have been used for many years attaining a height of $1^1/_2$ or 2 feet, and a diameter of 8 or 10 feet."

In the center of the mound is the burrow. It goes very nearly straight down; that is, *every Prairie-dog's burrow is a plunge hole*—a sheer drop for rapid escape from danger.

The main hole is generally $4^1/_2$ inches in diameter after it has left the funnel and narrowed to its normal calibre.

While one burrow to one mound is the rule, Mearns remarks of those he saw in Arizona: "A good many occupied burrows had no mounds whatever around them. I saw 3 adults enter a single burrow." Also, "there are often several burrows in each mound." These, however, are abnormalities. . . .

LIVES OF GAME ANIMALS, 1925–1927

Vulnerability

A Prairie-dog cannot see well unless he is sitting up on his hind legs; his eyes are of little use when he is nosing in the grass; and Tito [a female coyote] knew this. Further, a yellowish-gray animal on yellowish-gray landscape is invisible till it moves. Tito seemed to know that. So, without any attempt to crawl or hide, she walked gently up-wind toward the Prairie-dog. Upwind, not in order to prevent the Prairie-dog smelling her, but so that she could smell him, which came to the same thing. As soon as the Prairie-dog sat up with some food in his hand she froze into a statue. As soon as he dropped again to nose in the grass, she walked steadily nearer, watching his every move so that she might be motionless each time he sat up to see what his distant brothers were barking at. Once or twice he seemed alarmed by the calls of his friends, but he saw nothing and resumed his feeding. She soon cut the fifty yards down to ten, and the ten to five, and still was undiscovered. Then, when again the Prairie-dog dropped down to seek more fodder, she made a quick dash, and bore him off kicking and squealing. Thus does the angel of the pruning-knife lop off those that are heedless and foolishly indifferent to the advantages of society.

LIVES OF THE HUNTED, 1901

Weasel

The thugs of India claim to be devotees of the Goddess of Destruction; and profess, therefore, that it is their duty to kill as many human beings as possible. The Weasel is the Thug of the Wild World. While other animals may kill to excess for the gratification of appetite, the Weasels alone seem to revel in slaughter for its own sake, to find unholy joy in the horrors of dying squeak, final quiver, and wholesale destruction. Gifted with tremendous strength and activity; at home in the tree top, under the snow, on the earth, under ground, or in the water; keen of wits, tireless of wind and limb, insatiably cruel and madly courageous, they are all too well equipped for their chosen Herodian task.

The following adventure that I witnessed in 1897 is good evidence of the ferocity and courage of this animal: On September 5, I was out near Medora, N. Dak., with several men on a Wolf hunt. At night, as we were about to roll up in our blankets, a member of the party called out: "Say, Jack, there's a Pack-rat just run under your saddle." As a Pack-rat *(Neotoma)* is a notorious mischief-maker among leathers, Jack went over and gave his saddle a kick. Then we heard him gasping, swearing, and finally shouting for help. In the dim light we could see him dancing like a maniac and clutching at his throat. The campers all sat up and answered his calls for help with jeers and derision. "Look at Jack; he's got 'em again. Kill them, Jack; the air's full of them," etc.

A white bull-terrier with us now rushed forth growling, and seemed also to leap at the man's throat, then to shake himself. Now the man grew calm, and we learned that he had kicked out, not a Pack-rat, but a Long-tailed Weasel, which immediately attacked him. It ran up his legs a number of times, aiming at his throat. He had clutched it and cast it off again and again, but it had persisted, and might have done him serious injury but for the prompt assistance of the bull-terrier. The specimen is now in the Field Museum.

LIFE HISTORIES OF NORTHERN ANIMALS, 1909

The ermine—this one done for a mammal book—is simply the winter coloration of the weasel. In this case probably the longtail weasel.

Ernest Seton Thompson

INDIANS & WOODCRAFT

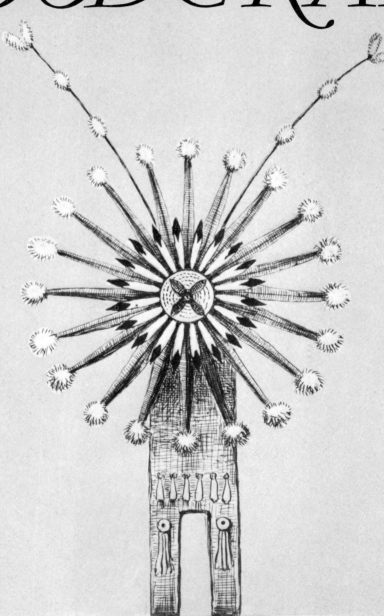

emembering the hungering-beyond-expression years of boyhood when there were no books from which to learn, it was natural to provide such texts for youngsters at the turn of the century. Perhaps it was the combination of the boyhood friendship with the Indian Chaska in Manitoba and years of reading about the monumental injustices wreaked upon the American Indian that prompted the Woodcraft Movement.

Years in the crowded East only served to emphasize the need to emulate the Indian and his culture. In a society where material gain seemed the goal of all, the Indian's sense of sharing had a strong appeal to a man of the earth. In a world of uncertainties and changing values, the Indian's time-tested creed appeared as a beacon to one seeking direction. Honor, courage, virtue, truth, physical health, and self-denial assumed greater proportions—particularly in the huge cities where one encountered deceit, subterfuge, weakness, and lies as a matter of daily course. Where morals seemed unimportant and abstinence an almost-forgotten word, the rigid disciplines of Indian life made their history all the more enviable.

No one read more history of Indian oppression in America. Friendship with Robert Valentine, commissioner of the Indian Bureau; Indian expert and writer George Bird Grinnell and historian Edgar Beecher Bronson provided the knowledge required to begin the establishment of a society patterned after the Red Man's way of life—if only for young boys.

The pages of the Indians' 200-year struggle against the whites filled him with a rage that was to last a lifetime. No one suffered more in reading of the slaughter of the remnants of Chief Joseph's Nez Percé tribe at the hands of the U.S. Cavalry in the 1890's. And no man wept more at the surrender words of that great chief.

"I am tired of fighting. Our chiefs are killed. Looking-Glass is dead. Toohulhulsote is dead. The old men are all dead. It is the young who say 'yes' or 'no.' He who led the young men is dead. It is cold and we have no blankets. The little children are freezing to death. My people, some of them, have run away to the hills and have no blankets, no food. No one knows where they are—perhaps freezing to death. I want to have time to look for my children and see how many of them I can find. Maybe I shall find them among the dead. Hear me, my chiefs. I am tired. My heart is sick and sad. From where the sun now stands I will fight no more forever."

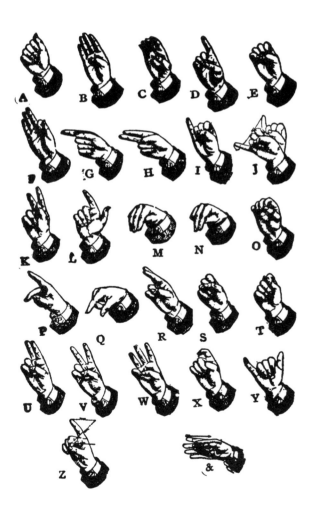

And when White Calf, chief of the Blackfeet, rushed into battle to save the life of Wolf Calf—outnumbered ten to one by his enemies the Crows and Gros Ventres—no heart beat faster in reading of it.

The injustices wrought upon Kanakuk, chief of the Kickapoos, when the administration of President Monroe ordered his people to leave their traditional fertile farmlands in Illinois and move into the rugged hills of Missouri, home of their lifelong enemies, the Osages, filled one with disgust at U.S. politics.

Tecumseh, chief of the Shawnee nation, remained an idol for a lifetime and personified all that was noble in the Indian. Being a Scot by birth and a citizen of Canada for many years may have had some bearing on a reverence for Tecumseh—particularly when he died, after having been commissioned a brigadier-general by the British Army in the War of 1812, fighting the American Army in the Battle of the Thames, at Moraviantown, Ontario.

But the vicious battles between the Cavalry and the Apaches, the Battle of Little Big Horn—from which there developed a lifelong hatred of George Armstrong Custer and all he stood for—paled into insignificance at the horror and anguish experienced in reading of the battles and final defeat of Dull Knife, chief of the Cheyennes.

After the Battle of Little Big Horn, the American Army rounded up a number of Indians who had played a part in that historic struggle. Some either could not or would not make an attempt to flee to the safety of Canada. Among the tribes rounded up were Dull Knife's warriors—who surrendered on the promise of fair treatment. But the administration of President Rutherford B. Hayes instructed the Army to march them

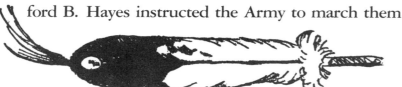

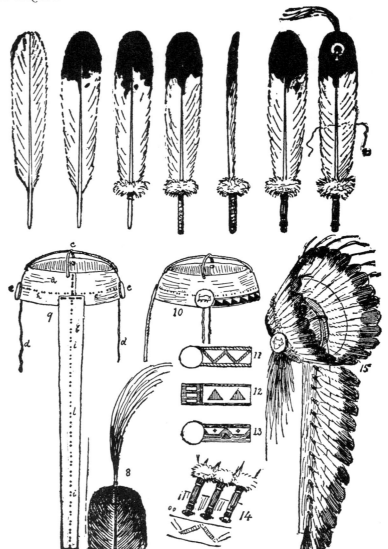

600 miles south of their home in the Black Hills of South Dakota to barren land in what was then simply called "Indian Territory." There, with promised rations never delivered and his people starving, Dull Knife saw his 235 warriors reduced to 69 by starvation and fever and his entire tribe of old men, women, and children dwindle to about 250 persons.

On September 9, 1878, Dull Knife—disillusioned

and angry—gathered his people together and headed for home, thus beginning one of the most heartbreaking treks in history. Two thousand troops set out in pursuit of Dull Knife and his band—the troops on fresh horses and supplied constantly by railroads and the U.S. Treasury. And in what must be a monument to heroism on one hand and brutality on the other, the weak warriors, women, and children fought the soldiers in as many as three pitched battles a week during the month it took the Cheyennes to reach the sparse haven of the Niobrara Sandhills across the South Platte River. They had no water and subsisted on the flesh of their horses, which they were forced to kill rather than starve. But on the fourteenth of October the bulk of the tribe, led as a ruse by a sub-chief, Little Wolf, evaded four fresh troops of Cavalry during the night and melted into the Black Hills, their ancestral home, to the north.

Dull Knife and his band of those less able to travel chose to decoy the Army and led them away from the main band. He sent word for help to the Sioux chief Red Cloud, but the Sioux had decided by then that it was useless to fight the administration in Washington—and ten days later the troops found Dull Knife and his survivors in the sandhills.

One would think the pitiful saga would have ended there—with the capture of the ragged, starved band, nearly out of ammunition and with but a few horses left. But Dull Knife and his people, after gaining strength from Army rations for a few days, suddenly fired on sentries from foxholes dug into the frozen ground with knives—until the Army battered them into a final surrender with field artillery brought in from Fort Robinson. Even in that surrender it was later discovered that twenty-two good rifles had been taken apart and were concealed beneath the clothing of squaws! When a more careful search was made some days later in a barracks where the remaining Cheyennes were held prisoner, the

guns and ammunition were found carefully hidden under the barracks floor. The band was kept under arrest at Fort Robinson while the Army tried to decide what to do with them. A council meeting was finally held in December which Red Cloud, Army generals, members of the Indian Bureau, and Dull Knife and his chiefs attended. The Sioux expressed sorrow at the plight of the Cheyennes but told Dull Knife the "Great Father" in Washington was all-powerful and his people filled the whole earth. He said the Sioux had asked Washington to allow the Cheyennes to come and live with them and that they would share with them. But he said there was much

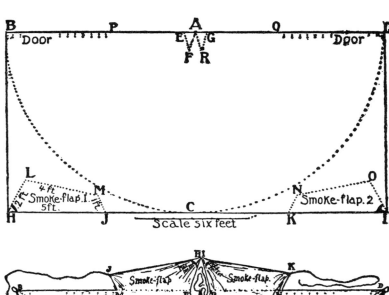

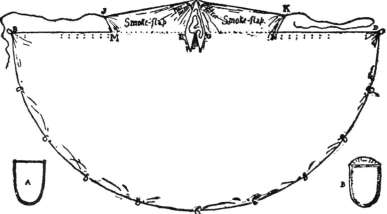

snow on the hills, ponies were thin, and game was scarce and urged his old friend to listen to what the Great Father ordered.

Dull Knife, then in his sixties, rose and thanked his brother. He said he hoped Washington would allow them to return to their homes, where they could live and hunt. He said he wanted no more war but he could not live in the south where there was no game. He said if Washington tried to send his people back they would butcher each other with their own knives.

On January 5 the answer came back. The War Department ordered the Army to return the Cheyennes to the Indian Territory in the south. Dull Knife and his chiefs were told of the order. The old man's body trembled with rage and he refused to leave the barracks. Five days later his people were half naked, without food or fires, but still holding out. A council was called, but two younger chiefs would not let Dull Knife attend, fearing a trap. The two young chiefs were then seized and placed in irons. In the struggle one of them, Wild Hog, stabbed a soldier and sounded his war cry as he did so. Believing it the end, the Indians began their war songs, barricaded the barracks windows and doors and dug up the rifles and ammunition. That day and the next night the Indians remained surrounded in the barracks until on the following night, shortly before midnight, in sub-zero cold, the Cheyennes made a break for freedom. Taken by surprise, the Army nevertheless quickly organized and set out in pursuit of the Indians, who were running afoot, carrying their horse bridles and lariats in hopes of finding horses. Had the warriors alone made a run for the heights they might have made it, but they chose to fight a rear-guard battle to cover women and children. More than half the fighting men fell in the first half mile of flight, women and children picking up the guns and fighting the troops themselves. Killed in the fighting were Dull Knife's daughter and his son Buffalo Hump.

At dawn four troops of Cavalry set out to gather survivors and found the remaining Cheyennes had followed a ridge between Soldier Creek and White River for ten miles and then had moved down to a narrow valley where their tracks could be followed in the snow. For seventeen miles from the Fort the tracks indicated the Cheyennes had not made a halt—old men, women, and half-starved children. The trail led to the top of a steep hill covered with blown-down timber and it was impossible for the troopers to travel except in single file. It was there the battered Cheyennes had dug in for yet another stand. At the burst of fire a number of soldiers fell from the saddles and the troops were stampeded into the brush.

The Indians maintained their stronghold that day and into the night. The following day troopers who tried to storm the hilltop could find only an occasional Cheyenne. They had concealed themselves in the snow, under dirty and torn strips of canvas, and blended into the background, but they continued to kill soldiers with devastating rifle fire. Charge after charge found individual warriors, their bare feet frozen, dead after having been hit half a dozen times and following a fight against overwhelming odds. Still without food on January 11,

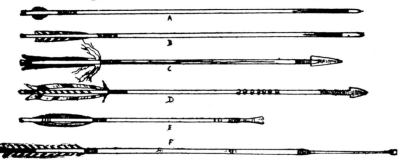

seven days after their escape, the Indians managed to keep up sniper fire from their hill. During that day they killed a trooper's horse and that night managed to cut off some of the meat for their first food in a week! With this food to help them gain strength, they held on for two more days, and when the troops again attacked they found the small band had managed to move six miles farther west, entrenched on Hat Creek Bluff—where they wounded two more troopers in an ambush. They resisted all efforts to dislodge them from this ground even though an artillery piece blasted forty rounds into their position. An interpreter and an officer crawled close to the position and called for the women and children to come out—promising them food, shelter, and protection. Certain now of the white man's intent, the Indians' answer was a volley of shots. The Cavalry troopers crawled back and surrounded the position as night came on. Incredible as it may seem, with dawn on the fourteenth, the soldiers found the Indians had slipped through the surrounding lines and had headed southwest along the high bluffs which bordered the basin of Hat Creek. For six more days there continued a running battle—the Indians were followed daily in a running fight, only to hole up at night, then slip out under the cover of darkness.

On Tuesday, January 21, 1879, came the final, agonizing finish. By this time the troops, numbering about 300, found the tiny band dug in a shallow wash near the headwaters of War Bonnet Creek, forty-four miles from where they had escaped from Fort Robinson on October 24. Worn out from fighting, without food and water and almost out of ammunition, the ragged band of thirty-four Cheyennes prepared to die as the hundreds of troopers advanced in skirmish order. Charging to the edge of the shallow ravine, still losing men to the sporadic fire, the soldiers fired volleys into the wash, sprang back to reload their carbines, and then rushed

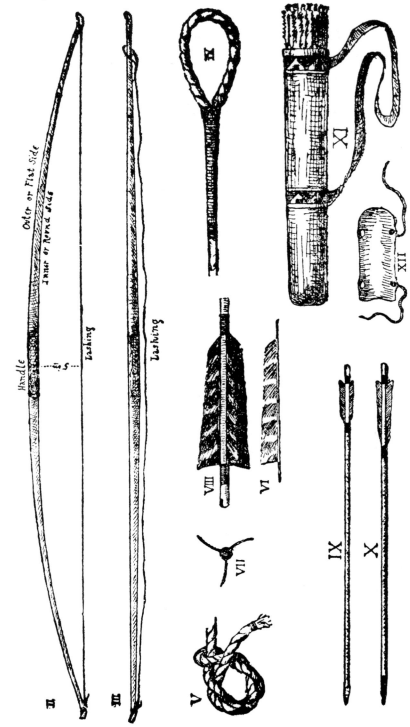

forward to fire again. Above the crash of rifles and pistols could be heard the death chants of the Cheyennes. At the last minute three warriors, one armed with an empty pistol and the other two carrying knives, rose from the pit and charged the hundreds of advancing cavalrymen! They were cut down by volleys of rifle fire and the fighting was finally over. Troopers removed twenty-two dead and nine wounded from the trench. All but two of the living—both women—were badly wounded.

And Dull Knife, wounded, captured, and turned over to the Ogalala Sioux to live out his days, sat stony-faced and spoke no more. Denied the right to die fighting with his people, he sat staring northward across the Badlands toward the faint blue haze that was the Black Hills, ancestral home of the Cheyennes.

And it was this that led to the books on Indians and woodcraft—after reading the horror stories of Indian massacres as a boy in his teens. It was the Battle of Wounded Knee and *On the Border with Crook,* reading Grinnell; *My Life as an Indian,* by J. W. Schultz; *Two Wilderness Voyagers,* by F. W. Calkins; *Famous Indian Chiefs I Have Known,* by General O. O. Howard; and the writing and paintings of George Catlin that inspired *Campfire Stories of Indian Character* and *The Spartans of the West,* published in *The Book of Woodcraft* in 1912. It was here that he found the words to express the anger, revulsion, and dread at the acts against the American Indian.

"As sure as there is a God in Heaven, this thing has to be met again, and for every drop of righteous blood spilled that day and on a thousand other days of like abomination, a fearful vengeance is being stored and will certainly break on us.

"As sure as Cain struck down himself when he murdered Abel; as sure as the blood of righteous Naboth cried from the ground and wrecked the house and the

kingdom and the race of Ahab; so surely has the American nation to stand before the bar of an earthly power—a power invincible, overwhelming, remorseless—and pay the uttermost price.

"As sure as this land was taken by fraud and held by cruelty and massacre, we have filled for ourselves a vial of

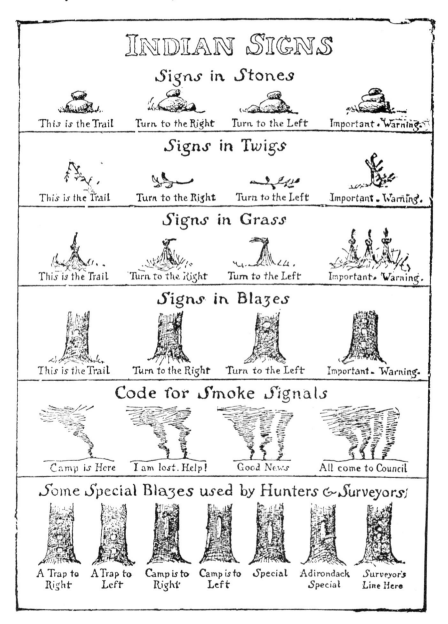

wrath. It will certainly be outpoured on us to the last drop and the dregs. What the Persian did to rich and rotten Babylon, what the Goth did to rich and bloody Rome, another race will surely do to us.

"If ever the aroused and reinspired Yellow man comes forth in his hidden strength, in his reorganized millions, overpowering, slaying, burning, possessing, we can only bow our heads and say, 'These are the instruments of God's wrath. We brought this on ourselves. All this we did to the Redman. The fate of Babylon and of bloody Rome is ours. We wrote our own doom as they did.' "

And so it was not unlikely that, to a middle-aged man living in the East—where there were innumerable problems of juvenile delinquency—the Indian way seemed an answer to troubled youth. Canadian youngsters years before had learned of woodcraft and nature as a part of growing up, and there seemed so much less delinquency looking back upon one's youth.

And as one read more of the Indians' creed: the acceptance of a Supreme Spirit; the immortality of the Soul; the body as the temple of the spirit; the domination of the body by fasting; reverence of parents and the old; the sacredness of property; cleanliness; morality; truth; beautification; the simple life; the obligations of hospitality; peace. The noblest of virtues is courage and the fear of death shall never enter the heart . . . to what more could a youngster—or, for that matter, an adult—aspire?

There was a wealthy man from New York who, wanting to do something for boys from the slum sections of the city, took a number of boys on an outing to the Catskills. Upon arriving there he waved at the woods and told the youngsters to go and enjoy themselves. Bewildered, the boys wandered aimlessly into the trees and the man left happy that he had done a fine thing. Imagine his disappointment when he returned to find them all seated beneath the trees, smoking, shooting

crap, and playing cards. What were they supposed to do? They neither knew nor understood nature, were ill at ease with the unknown, and fell back upon what they usually did for recreation in the crowded city.

But a man from the land knew. When boys were in trouble, caused mischief—as they did in painting his gates and defacing his property at Cos Cob—what better way to keep idle hands busy than to organize them into an Indian society? From a modest start with the handful of pranksters, there grew an organization—the Woodcraft Indians—whose charter and by-laws were published first in the *Ladies' Home Journal,* 1902.

There was a genuine desire to shape the lives of youngsters—particularly boys from homes where there had never been any exposure to the world of nature. From the Woodcraft Indians came the *Birchbark Roll*s published annually by Doubleday, Page & Company from 1903 to 1916. Out of the handful of Seton's Woodcraft Indians there grew the Woodcraft League of America and *Manual of the Woodcraft Indians.*

It was natural that—as a lecturer and writer—there should be the trips to England and Europe, where many lectures were given on the new boys' movement which was founded on an Indian movement. In the manual there were rules for behavior, cleanliness, dances, first aid, honors, nature study, songs, pottery making, weaving, fasting, sleeping outdoors, and outdoor cookery—all patterned after the Indian way.

There were the discussions with educators in Boston who believed it was a movement which would soon be worldwide. In 1904 there were dozens of talks on the movement in England alone—and where, in the same year, several camps were formed at Eccles, Hove, New Brighton, and Kent Hatch and the *Birchbark Roll* was distributed as the official manual.

No. 1.   No. 2.   No. 3.   No. 4.   No. 5.   No. 6.   No. 7.   No. 8.

And later—after the meetings in 1906 with Lord Baden-Powell at the Savoy in London, where Baden-Powell asked for more information on the youth organization—Baden-Powell rewrote his brochure *Aids to Scouting* as a handbook for Church Lads, a British religious organization. It was primarily a military type of organization, based upon military drill of the British Army, and the group became known as the Boy Scouts. There were letters. . . . January 24, 1908: "You will infer from the above address that we are going on with my scheme like your 'Woodcraft Indians.' And it promises well. I hope that you will allow me to make frequent mention of yourself and your tribes as examples to the Scouts." February 13, 1908: "I wrote to you the other day in America, telling you how I had been able to make a start with my scheme of scouting for boys, much on the line of your Woodcraft Indians, and sending you the handbook. . . ."

And when Baden-Powell's *Scouting for Boys* appeared for the first time in 1908 there was anger and hurt to find the ideas and games appropriated and given new names with no word of acknowledgment. In answer to a letter there was, on March 14, 1908: "Thank you very much for your kind letter. I much regret that I should have omitted mentioning the source of several of the games as being taken from your 'Birchbark Roll,' but the truth is, I made a general statement to that effect in the introduction to the book, which I afterwards cut from the beginning [and] have inserted it at the end, where you will see it in Part VI. But in doing this I had not reflected that the remarks, giving the authorship of the games, would not be read by the people until after the games had appeared before them. I very much regret this oversight, and it is most kind of you to have taken it in the good natured way in which you have done."

No such acknowledgment was ever made and there were later the recriminations and a feeling of bitterness over a need to squabble about a movement that had been designed to help youngsters. And in the following years there was much more bitterness and the Boy Scout movement was moved to America and set up along military lines—with uniforms, drill, and officers as well as the motto "Be Prepared." With misgivings the new manual was written for American boys—incorporating the military scout nomenclature—and there was the affiliation with the organization, as Chief Scout, until 1915. At that time politics grew in the organization and as the movement also expanded and revenue exceeded $3 million, it became big business. There were power struggles and bickering with Daniel Carter Beard, another woodsman and an energetic promoter, and Scout officials such as Executive Secretary James E. West. The result was leaving the Scout movement completely in 1915.

But the ideal remained, based upon Indian lore, causing a brief revival; there was an attempt to establish *The Red Lodge,* and later to become an active leader of the Camp Fire Club of America—for those who would organize groups of youngsters over the age of eighteen—but close friends advised against it, for reasons best known to themselves, and perhaps to the gods of the Red Man.

And on to the end of the days of a life—unswerving in its goals and uncompromising in its intent—there was the identification with all that was fine about the Indian. In the last years, as Navajos, Hopis, and the many Indians of the Pueblo tribes of the Rio Grande Valley paid true homage to the man they honestly called The Chief, there was never a doubt of the truth of Indian ways.

In the visits to the grave of Sitting Bull and in the interviews with Big Nose, in the rhythmic beat of the Pueblo corn dance and watching the Hopi Shalako wooden heads crossing the river at dusk—the mammoth wooden bird heads grotesque in the half light of dusk against the sandstone cliffs—there remained the conviction that the Indian belief was the best.

For in the mind of an old man—shouting into the winds of a global war which engulfed us all until no one cared for the history of the Indian movement or the ways of woodcraft—there was very little difference between a slum boy learning to be brave, clean, and reverent, and the despair of Dull Knife, staring mute at the faint line that was the Black Hills . . . ancestral home of the Cheyennes.

JOHN G. SAMSON

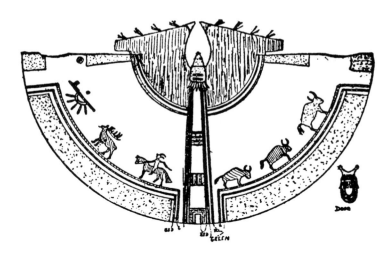

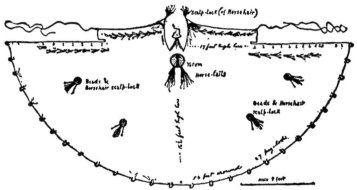

Cabin

I was fourteen years of age when I began to build it. During most of the year 1874 it was in progress. In the spring of 1875 I found unmeasured happiness in going there Saturdays alone.

I gathered shells, feathers, curios in the woods, and arranged them on little shelves. I imagined myself Robinson Crusoe and Swiss Family Robinson rolled into one. I hoped some day to re-establish Indian life in some form. I played Indian, ran about without anything on but my boots, so as to get sunburned brown. An old putty knife was ground on a grindstone into the correct form for a hunting or scalping knife. I made a leather case for it to hang at my belt; and

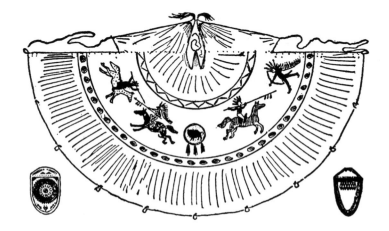

although disfigured by the glazier's notch, it gave me joy, and served as my knife till I lost it eight years later in the Sandhills of Manitoba.

I made myself a pair of moccasins of some old sheep leather. They did not last more than two or three days, but they were magic moccasins to me. I stuck feathers in my hair, and cultivated an Indian accent. I adopted an Indian vocabulary. "White man heap no good" was a favorite phrase.

I longed for a companion and confidant of like tastes. My brother next older was possible, but not reliable. He might join in with mild enthusiasm, or he might scoff at the whole thing as foolishness. Besides, he was not free, being at work. Saturday afternoons he had, but had decided to give the time to music lessons. So I kept my secret to myself.

TRAIL OF AN ARTIST-NATURALIST, 1940

Chipewyans

Sweeping generalisations are always misleading, therefore I offer some now, and later will correct them by specific instances. These Chipewyans are dirty, shiftless, improvident, and absolutely honest. Of the last we saw daily instances in crossing the country. Valuables hung in trees, protected only from weather, birds, and beasts, but never a suggestion that they needed protection from mankind. They are kind and hospitable among themselves, but grasping in their dealings with white men, as already set forth. While they are shiftless and lazy, they also undertake the frightful toil of hunting and portaging. Although improvident, they have learned to dry a stock of meat and put up a scaffold of white fish for winter use. As a tribe they are mild and inoffensive, although they are the original stock from which the Apaches broke away some hundreds of years ago before settling in the south.

They have suffered greatly from diseases imported by white men, but not from whiskey. The Hudson's Bay Company has always refused to supply liquor to the natives. What little of the evil traffic there has been was the work of free-traders. But the Royal Mounted Police have most rigorously and effectually suppressed this. Nevertheless, Chief Trader Anderson tells me that the Mackenzie Valley tribes have fallen to less than half their numbers during the last century.

It is about ten years since they made the treaty that surrendered their lands to the government. They have no reserves, but are free to hunt as their fathers did.

I found several of the older men lamenting the degeneracy of their people. "Our fathers were hunters and our mothers

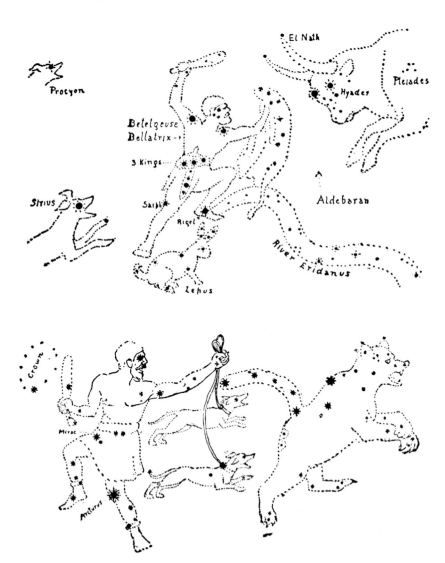

made good moccasins, but the young men are lazy loafers around the trading posts, and the women get money in bad ways to buy what they should make with their hands."

The Chipewyan dialects are peculiarly rasping, clicking, and guttural, especially when compared with Cree.

Every man and woman and most of the children among them smoke. They habitually appear with a pipe in their mouth and speak without removing it, so that the words gurgle out on each side of the pipe while a thin stream goes sizzling through the stem. This additional variant makes it hopeless to suggest on paper any approach to their peculiar speech.

The Jesuits tell me that it was more clicked and guttural fifty years ago, but that they are successfully weeding out many of the more unpleasant catarrhal sounds.

In noting down the names of animals, I was struck by the fact that the more familiar the animal the shorter its name. Thus the Beaver, Muskrat, Rabbit, and Marten, on which they live, are respectively Tsa, Dthen, Ka, and Tha. The less familiar (in a daily sense) Red Fox and Weasel are Nak-ee-they, Noon-dee-a, Tel-ky-lay; and the comparatively scarce Musk-ox and little Weasel, At-huh-le-ker-ray and Tel-ky-lay-azzy. All of which is clear and logical, for the name originally is a description, but the softer parts and sharp angles are worn down by the attrition of use—the more use they have for a word the shorter it is bound to get. In this connection it is significant that "to-day" is To-ho-chin-nay, and "to-morrow" Kom-pay.

The Chipewyan teepee is very distinctive; fifty years ago all were of caribou leather, now most are of cotton; not for lack of caribou, but because cotton does not need continual watching to save it from the dogs. Of the fifty teepees at Fort Chipewyan, one or two only were of caribou but many had caribou-skin tops, as these are less likely to burn than those of cotton.

The way they manage the smoke is very clever; instead of the two fixed flaps, as among the Plains River Indians, these have a separate hood which is easily set on any side. Chief Squirrel lives in a lodge that is an admirable combination of the white men's tent with its weather-proof roof and the Indian teepee with its cosy fire.

Not one of these lodges that I saw, here or elsewhere, had the slightest suggestion of decoration.

For people who spend their whole life on or near the water these are the worst boatmen I ever saw. The narrow, thick paddle they make, compared with the broad, thin Iroquois paddle, exactly expressed the difference between the two as canoemen. The Chipewyan's mode of using it is to sit near the middle and make 2 or perhaps 3 strokes on one side, then change to the other side for the same, and so on. The line made by the canoes is an endless zigzag. The idea of paddling on one side so dexterously that the canoe goes straight is yet on an evolutionary pinnacle beyond their present horizon.

In rowing, their way is to stand up, reach forward with the 30-pound $16\frac{1}{2}$-foot oar, throw all the weight on it, falling backward into the seat. After half an hour of this exhausting work they must rest 15 to 20 minutes. The long, steady, strong pull is unknown to them in every sense.

Their ideas of sailing a boat are childish. Tacking is like washing, merely a dim possibility of their very distant future. It's a sailing wind if behind; otherwise it's a case of furl and row.

By an ancient, unwritten law the whole country is roughly divided among the hunters. Each has his own recognized hunting ground, usually a given river valley, that is his exclusive and hereditary property; another hunter may follow a wounded animal into it, but not begin a hunt there or set a trap upon it.

Most of their time is spent at the village, but the hunting ground is visited at proper seasons.

Fifty years ago they commonly went half naked. How they stood the insects I do not

know, and when asked they merely grinned significantly; probably they doped themselves with grease.

This religious training has had one bad effect. Inspired with horror of being "naked" savages, they do not run any sinful risks, even to take a bath. In all the six months I was among them I never saw an Indian's bare arms, much less his legs. One day after the fly season was over I took advantage of the lovely weather and water to strip off and jump into a lake by our camp; my Indians modestly turned their backs until I had finished. If this mock modesty worked for morality one might well accept it, but the old folks say that it operates quite the other way. It has at all events put an end to any possibility of them taking a bath. Maybe as a consequence, but of this I am not sure, none of these Indians swim. A large canoe-load upset in crossing Great Slave Lake a month after we arrived and all were drowned.

Like most men who lead physical lives, and like all meat-eating savages, these are possessed of a natural proneness toward strong drink. An interesting two-edged boomerang illustration of this was given by an unscrupulous whiskey trader. While travelling across country he ran short of provisions but fortunately came to a Chipewyan lodge. At first its owner had no meat to spare, but when he found that the visitor had a flask of whiskey he offered for it a large piece of Moose meat; when this was refused he doubled the amount, and after another refusal added some valuable furs and more meat till one hundred dollars worth was piled up.

Again the answer was "no."

Then did that Indian offer the lodge and everything he had in it, including his wife. But the trader was obdurate.

"Why didn't you take it," said the friend whom he told of the affair; "the stuff would have netted five hundred dollars, and all for one flask of whiskey."

"Not much," said the trader, "it was my last flask. I wouldn't 'a' had a drop for myself. But it just shows how fond these Indians are of whiskey." THE ARCTIC PRAIRIES, 1911

Indians

O f all the figures in the light of Indian history, that of Tecumseh, or Tecumtha the "Leaping Panther," the war chief of the Shawnees, stands out perhaps highest and best as the ideal, noble Redman.

His father was chief of the tribe. Tecumseh was born in 1768 at Piqua Indian Village, near the site of Springfield, Ohio. Of all the Indians, the Shawnees had been most energetic and farseeing in their opposition to the encroachments of the whites. But the flood of invasion was too strong for them. The old chief fell, battling for home and people, at Point Pleasant, in 1774. His eldest son followed the father's footsteps, and the second met death in a hopeless fight with Wayne in 1794, leaving young Tecumseh war chief of his tribe. At once he became a national figure. He devoted his whole life and strength to the task of saving his people from the invaders, and to that end resolved that he must effect a national federation of the Redmen. Too often tribe had been pitted against tribe for the white men's advantage. In union alone he

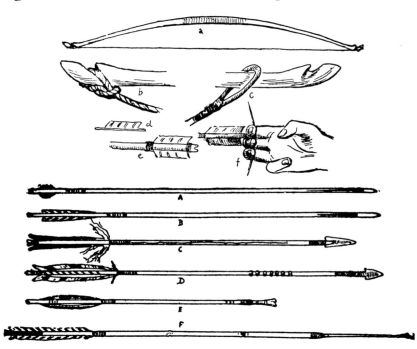

saw the way of salvation and to this end he set about an active campaign among the tribes of the Mississippi Valley.

His was no mean spirit of personal revenge; his mind was too noble for that. He hated the whites as the destroyers of his race, but prisoners and the defenseless knew well that they could rely on his honor and humanity and were safe under his protection. When only a boy—for his military career began in childhood—he had witnessed the burning of a prisoner, and the spectacle was so abhorrent to his feelings that by an earnest and eloquent harangue he induced the party to give up the practice forever. In later years his name was accepted by helpless women and children as a guarantee of protection even in the midst of hostile Indians. He was of commanding figure, nearly six feet in height and compactly built; of dignified bearing and piercing eye, before whose lightning even a British general quailed. His was the fiery eloquence of a Clay and the clear-cut logic of a Webster. Abstemious in habit, charitable in thought and action, he was brave as a lion, but humane and generous withal—in a word, an aboriginal American knight-errant, whose life was given to his people.

During the four years 1807 to 1811 he went from tribe to tribe urging with all his splendid powers the need for instant and united resistance.

His younger brother, Tenskwatawa the Prophet, was with him and helped in his way by preaching the regenerated doctrine of the Indian life. The movement was gaining force. But all Tecumseh's well-laid plans were frustrated by the premature battle of Tippecanoe, November 7, 1811. In this his brother, the Prophet, was defeated and every prospect of an Indian federation ended for the time.

The War of 1812 gave Tecumseh a chance to fight the hated Americans. As a British general he won many battles for his allies, but was killed leading his warriors at Moraviantown, near Chatham, Ontario, on October 5, 1813. His personal prowess, his farseeing statesmanship, his noble eloquence, and lofty character have given him a place on the very highest plane among patriots and martyrs.

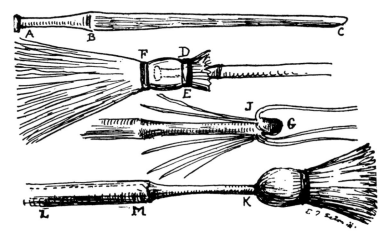

If ever the great Hiawatha was reincarnated it must have been in the form of Tecumseh. Like Hiawatha, he devoted his whole life to the service of his people on the most heroic lines. Like Hiawatha, he planned a national federation of all Redmen that should abolish war among themselves and present a solid front to the foreign invader. "America for the Americans" was his cry, and all his life and strength were devoted to the realization of his dream. Valiant as Pontiac, wise as Metacomet, magnificent as Powhatan, kind and gentle as the young Winona, he was a farther-seeing statesman than they ever had had before, and above all was the first leading Redman to put an end to the custom for which they chiefly are blamed, the torturing of prisoners. His people were always kind to their own; his great soul made him kind to all the world. He fought his people's battles to the end, and when he knew the cause was lost he laid aside his British uniform, girded himself in his Indian war-chief dress for the final scene, bade good-bye to his men and went forth, like King Saul on Mt. Gilboa's fatal field, to fight and fighting die. And the Star of his race had set.

Measured by any scale, judged by any facts, there can be but one verdict: He was a great man, an Indian without guile, a mighty soldier and statesman, loved and revered by all who knew him. More than a Red nobleman, he was acclaimed by all his kin who knew his life as in very truth a Son of God.

THE BOOK OF WOODCRAFT AND INDIAN LORE, 1912

BIBLIOGRAPHY

Note: Titles have been listed in order of their publication.

Studies in the Art Anatomy of Animals
New York, Macmillan, 1896

Wild Animals I Have Known
New York, Scribner's, 1898

Lobo, Rag, and Vixen
New York, Scribner's, 1899

Trail of the Sandhill Stag
New York, Scribner's, 1899

The Biography of a Grizzly
New York, Century, 1900

Lives of the Hunted
New York, Scribner's, 1901

Two Little Savages
New York, Doubleday, 1903

Monarch, the Big Bear of Tallac
New York, Scribner's, 1904

Animal Heroes
New York, Scribner's, 1905

Woodmyth and Fable
New York, Century, 1905

*The Natural History
of the Ten Commandments*
New York, Scribner's, 1907

Life Histories of Northern Animals
(2 volumes) New York, Scribner's, 1909

The Biography of a Silver-Fox
New York, Century, 1909

Boy Scouts of America Official Manual*
New York, 1910

Rolf in the Woods
Garden City, Doubleday, 1911

Arctic Prairies
New York, Scribner's, 1911

Wild Animals at Home
Garden City, Doubleday, 1913

The Slum Cat
London, Constable, 1915

Legend of the White Reindeer
London, Constable, 1915

Wild Animal Ways
Garden City, Doubleday, 1916

Preacher of Cedar Mountain
New York, Doubleday, 1917

Sign Talk
New York, Doubleday, 1918

Woodland Tales
Garden City, Doubleday, 1921

Bannertail, the Story of a Gray Squirrel
New York, Scribner's, 1922

Library of Pioneering and Woodcraft
New York, Doubleday, 1925
(six books in a matching set)

Lives of Game Animals
(4 volumes) Garden City, Doubleday, 1925–27
(sometimes issued as four volumes in eight parts)

Old Silver Grizzly
London, Hodder and Stoughton, 1927

Raggylug and Other Stories
London, Hodder and Stoughton, 1927

Katug, the Snow Child
London, Blackwell, 1927

Chink and Other Stories
London, Hodder and Stoughton, 1927

Foam, the Razorback
London, Hodder and Stoughton, 1927

Johnny Bear and Other Stories
London, Hodder and Stoughton, 1927

Lobo and Other Stories
London, Hodder and Stoughton, 1927

Krag, the Kootenay Ram and Other Stories
London, University of London Press, 1929

Billy, the Dog That Made Good
London, Hodder and Stoughton, 1930

Cute Coyote and Other Stories
London, Hodder and Stoughton, 1930

Lobo; Bingo and the Racing Mustang
n.p., State, 1930

Gospel of the Redman
(with Julia Seton) New York, Doubleday, 1936

Great Historic Animals
New York, Scribner's, 1937

The Biography of an Arctic Fox
New York, Appleton-Century, 1937

Trail of an Artist Naturalist
(autobiography) New York, Scribner's, 1940

Santana, the Hero Dog of France
n.p., Phoenix Press, 1945
(500 numbered copies, 300 autographed)

*In 1910, the Boy Scouts of America printed two "official"
handbooks. Ernest Thompson Seton and Lieutenant General
Sir Robert S. S. Baden-Powell, K. C. B., are given as authors on
the cover of the first printing. Although only Seton's name appears
on the cover of the second printing, with the title "Chief Scout,"
both names are listed on the title page of each printing.